Edited by Alfred H. Barr, Jr.

PICASSO

75th ANNIVERSARY EXHIBITION

THE MUSEUM OF MODERN ART, NEW YORK *May 22—September 8, 1957*

THE ART INSTITUTE OF CHICAGO *October 29—December 8, 1957*

Published by the Museum of Modern Art, New York

FRONTISPIECE: *Girl Writing*. 1934. Oil on canvas, 63⅞ x 51⅜. Florene and Samuel Marx, Chicago

Please insert in your copy of

PICASSO: 75TH ANNIVERSARY EXHIBITION CATALOGUE
THE MUSEUM OF MODERN ART, NEW YORK

Additions and Corrections

Page

11 and 16 For Museo de Arte Moderno, Madrid, read Museo Nacional de Arte Moderno, Madrid

42 *Guitar:* for (Spring 1912), read 1913

44 *Man with Hat,* not included in New York exhibition

46 *Portrait of a Girl,* not included in exhibition

55 *Four Bathers,* not included in exhibition

60 *Paul as Pierrot,* dated on the back 28 February 1925

75-78 *Guernica* studies and "postscripts": omitted from the New York exhibition are the following: (Early May 1937?), *Horse and Bull;* 28 May, *Weeping head;* 3 June, *Head and horse's hoofs;* 15 June, both *Weeping heads;* 22 June, *Weeping head with handkerchief;* (4) July, *Weeping head with handkerchief;* 26 September, *Mother with dead child;* 13 October, *Weeping head with handkerchief;* 17 October, *Weeping woman with handkerchief*

82 *Portrait of D. M.* (Paris): for oil, read oil on canvas

86 *Woman in Gray:* for oil on canvas, read oil on wood

93 *Still Life:* presented to Matisse, 1944

97 For *Chimneys of Vallauris,* read *Smoke at Vallauris*

101 For the two *Little Owls,* the captions have been reversed; read caption 1 for the right, caption 2 for the center reproduction

104 *Mme H. P.* Vallauris: for 30 July 1952, read 30 September 1952

105 *Chinese Commode:* for oil on canvas, read oil on wood

108-109 *Les Femmes d'Alger:* canvases "B", "D", and "I" omitted from New York exhibition for lack of space

Additional Works Shown in New York

Flower Girl. (1906). Ink, 24⅞ x 19″. The Museum of Modern Art, gift of Mrs. Stanley B. Resor

Landscape. 1920. (Zervos Volume IV). Oil on canvas, 20½ x 27½″. The artist

Three Women at the Spring. 1921. (Zervos Volume IV). Oil on canvas, 80¼ x 68½″. The Museum of Modern Art, gift of Mr. and Mrs. Allan D. Emil

Thursday. Vallauris, 14 June 1951. Oil on plywood, 41¼ x 53⅞″. The artist

Corrections in Measurements

Page

14 *Gypsy Girl:* size should read 17½ x 23½″

17 *Dwarf Dancer (La Nana):* size should read 41⅝ x 23¾″

26 *Head of a Girl:* size should read 5⅜″; *Head of a Jester:* size should read 15″

28 *Peasants from Andorra:* size should read 27⅞ x 16½″ (sight)

29 *Self Portrait:* size should read 36½ x 28¾″

39 *Wilhelm Uhde:* size should read 32 x 23¾″

45 *Woman in an Armchair:* size should read 59¼ x 39⅜″

55 *Nude seated on a Rock:* size should read 6¼ x 4⅜″

58 *Mandolin on a Table:* size should read 32½ x 39⅜″

67 *Pitcher and Bowl of Fruit:* size should read 51¼ x 64″

74 *Woman with Hat:* size should read 23⅝ x 19¼″; *Portrait of D. M.* (Paris): size should read 25¼ x 20¼″

79 *Weeping Woman:* size should read 24 x 19⅝″

82 *Jaime Sabartés:* size should read 18⅛ x 15″; *Portrait of D. M.* (Paris): size should read 36⅛ x 28⅝″

84 *Still Life with Sausage:* size should read 36⅛ x 25⅝″

97 *Sport of Pages:* size should read 21¼ x 25½″

100 CENTER: *Owl.* Size should read 13⅜″

101 LEFT: *Angry Owl.* Size should read 12⅞″

107 *The Studio (Painter and Model):* size should read 13⅞ x 10⅜″

110 *The Studio:* size should read 74⅞ x 31½″

112 *Woman in Rocking Chair:* size should read 76⅞ x 51⅛″

114 *Woman by a Window:* size should read 63⅞ x 51¼″

PREFACE AND ACKNOWLEDGMENTS

Picasso was seventy-five years old last October. This exhibition, organized by the Museum of Modern Art with the support of the Art Institute of Chicago and the Philadelphia Museum of Art, contributes to the celebration of his anniversary.

The exhibition was originally planned to show Picasso's art since his *Guernica* mural of 1937. It would thus simply have supplemented the retrospective Picasso show of 1939. However, since 1939 a whole new generation has come to maturity. For its sake and to make possible a comparative study of Picasso's art throughout his prodigious career, the scope of the exhibition has been extended to include some sixty years of work.

Though the period covered is half again as long, the present survey is not so systematically comprehensive as that of 1939. For lack of space, certain media, notably prints and ceramics, have been entirely omitted. This has made room for the largest showing in America of Picasso's rather neglected sculpture and a generous number of drawings. Most of the important sculptures so far released by the artist, as well as many lesser works, are included. Had the many major pieces still in Picasso's possession been available (as was expected), the artist would, I believe, have been revealed as one of the great sculptors of our time. His brilliance and power as a draftsman are demonstrated by the seventy drawings selected from American collections by William S. Lieberman.

Picasso's American amateurs will find many well-known canvases in the exhibition. This was inevitable, since it seemed essential to include certain capital paintings no matter how familiar. Besides, in the novel context of unaccustomed and challenging neighbors, even the often-seen canvas may display unexpected qualities.

Many paintings and drawings have never before been exhibited in America. Some in fact are almost unknown even to students of Picasso. For instance the *Woman in Blue*, page 16, was shown at the Madrid Bellas Artes exhibition of 1901 and may even be the first Picasso to enter a public museum, yet it languished for nearly fifty years almost forgotten and quite unpublished until recently. Painted perhaps in the same year, the *Self Portrait*, page 13, has, it appears, never before been reproduced. It was bought in 1911 from the Thannhauser Gallery, Munich, by Hugo von Hofmannsthal with royalties from his libretto for *Der Rosenkavalier*. In 1907, while he was at work on *Les Demoiselles d'Avignon*, Picasso painted an elaborate and unique composition in full fauve color, *The Harvesters*, page 32, which he gave to his old friend, Sebastián Junyer, of Barcelona, where the painting remained until last year. The *Jug and Bowl*, page 32, Picasso gave to Matisse in 1907-08, repeating the gesture almost forty years later with a still life of 1944, page 93. Both are published here apparently for the first time.

The exhibition welcomes four of the most notable cubist pictures to this country, the *Girl with Mandolin*, page 38, recently acquired by a New York collector, and three loans not seen here before, the *Aficionado*, from the Basle Museum, page 41, the *Woman in an Armchair*, page 45, and the *Portrait of a Girl*, page 46, the last lent by that admirable connoisseur of twentieth-century art, the Director of the National Museums of France. With these should be mentioned the exquisite oval still life, page 44, from the collection of the National Gallery of Norway.

At the heart of the cubist section may be found a concentration of collages, pages 42-44, rivaled in number only by the neo-classic "miniatures" of the early 1920s, pages 54-55. By contrast with these two groups, the large number of portraits was quite unplanned. The famous portrait of Sebastián Junyer, page 18; the youthful self portraits, pages 13, 17 and 29; the artist's early patrons, Leo and Gertrude Stein, page 29, Wilhelm Uhde, page 39, and Dr. Claribel Cone, page 54; two of his pioneer dealers, Daniel-Henry Kahnweiler, page 39, and Ambroise Vollard, page 48; Diaghilev, who commissioned most of his ballet designs, page 48; the charming portrayals of his children, Paul, page 60, Maya, page 82, and Claude, page 98; the affectionate if vertiginous mask of his faithful friend and biographer, Jaime Sabartés, page 82; the formidable intensity of his little daughter Paloma at play, page 99; the witty bravura of the two portraits of Madame H.P., page 104, and the proud profile of Jacqueline Roque, page 110; all these images of friends offer evidence that, as in the past, the greatest portraits were painted by the greatest artists rather than by specialists.

The largest number of works previously unseen in America date of course from the most recent third of Picasso's career, the period since *Guernica*. Besides the portraits reviewed above, one may take special note of the famous pair of still lifes with a bull's head, page 81, the large *Serenade*, lent by the Musée d'Art Moderne, the bitterly humorous cycle of drawings, pages 106-107, the fifteen variations on a theme by Delacroix, pages 9 and 108-109, the little view of Vallauris with smoke pouring from its ceramic furnaces, page 97, and, dating from last year, the large seated figures and studio interiors, pages 110-114, works which bear witness to the sustained invention and vitality of the artist now in his 75th year, the man who by a coincidence of anniversaries, can look back exactly 20 years to his *Guernica* and 50 years to *Les Demoiselles d'Avignon*.

ACKNOWLEDGMENTS

The recent triumphal procession of large Picasso retrospective exhibitions began in the museums of Rome and Milan in 1953, followed by Lyons and São Paulo in 1954, and the series of 75th birthday exhibitions in Paris and Munich in 1955, Cologne, Hamburg, Moscow and Oslo in 1956. The consequent and very natural exhaustion of lenders (not to mention the works of art!) have added to the already very great sense of gratitude and indebtedness felt by the three American museums toward those whose generosity and collaboration have contributed to the exhibition.

First of all, on behalf of the Trustees of The Art Institute of Chicago, The Philadelphia Museum of Art* and The Museum of Modern Art, we should like to thank M. Pablo Picasso for his support of the exhibition and his loan of no less than thirty works in addition to the *Guernica* mural and its studies.

Picasso's representative, M. Daniel-Henry Kahnweiler and his associates of the Galerie Louise Leiris, particularly Mme Leiris herself, and M. Maurice Jardot have been most self-sacrificing in working with both Picasso and the Museum of Modern Art during the very difficult period when the gallery was moving to a new location and opening its own show of Picasso's recent painting. Mr. Kahnweiler, scholar, dealer and one of Picasso's staunchest champions, is, in this season of anniversaries, celebrating his 50th year of association with the artist. In New York, Mr. and Mrs. Daniel Saidenberg of the Saidenberg Gallery, helpful in many ways, have been particularly considerate in postponing their exhibition of Picasso's latest paintings so that it would not anticipate the Museum's show.

Besides the generous lenders who are listed on pages 8, 11, we cordially thank the following:

—for their help in securing loans from museums: Mr. Gordon M. Smith, Director, The Albright Art Gallery, Buffalo; Mrs. Adelyn D. Breeskin, Director, and Miss Gertrude Rosenthal, Senior Curator, The Baltimore Museum of Art; Mr. Charles Nagel, Director, and Mr. William N. Eisendrath, Jr., Assistant Director, The City Art Museum of St. Louis; Professor Wolfgang Stechow, The Dudley Peter Allen Memorial Art Museum, Oberlin College; Mr. John Coolidge, Director, The Fogg Art Museum, Harvard University; Mr. Arnold Rüdlinger, Curator, Kunsthalle, Basle; Dr. R. Wehrli, Director, Kunsthaus, Zürich; Dr. Georg Schmidt, Director, Kunstmuseum, Basle; M. Georges A. Salles, Director, The Louvre and the National Museums of France; Mr. James J. Rorimer, Director, and Mr. Theodore Rousseau, Curator of Paintings, The Metropolitan Museum of Art, New York; M. Jean Cassou, Chief Curator, and M. Bernard Dorival, Curator, Musée National d'Art Moderne, Paris; Don Enrique Lafuente y Ferrari, Director, Museo de Arte Moderno, Madrid; Dr. Sigurd Willoch, Director, and Mr. Leif Oestby, Keeper, Nasjonalgalleriet, Oslo; Mrs. Ala Story, Director, The Santa Barbara Museum of Art; Mr. Blake-More Godwin, Director, The Toledo Museum of Art; Mr. John Reid of the Cultural Affairs Offices, U. S. Embassy, Madrid; Mr. Charles C. Cunningham, Director, The Wadsworth Atheneum, Hartford

—for their help in securing loans from private owners: Dr. P. Bouffard, Director, Musée d'Art et d'Histoire, Geneva; Mme Marie Cuttoli; Mr. Niels Ebbesen; Mr. Victor W. Ganz; Mr. Otto M. Gerson; Mr. Pierre Matisse; Mr. Klaus Perls; Miss

*The Philadelphia Museum will open the exhibition, with certain changes, in January, 1958.

Joyce Reeves; Mr. John Rewald; Mr. Per Rom; Mr. Paul Rosenberg; Mr. Jaime Sabartés; Mr. Sam Salz; Mr. and Mrs. Javier Vilato

—for their help in providing information or photographs: Mr. Sidney Janis; Mr. Henry Kleemann; Dr. Otto Kallir; M. Knoedler & Co.; Mr. and Mrs. Samuel M. Kootz; Prof. José Lopez-Rey; Mr. Frederick Mayor; Mr. and Mrs. Roland Penrose; Mr. Antoni Ribera; Mr. Germain Seligman; Mr. James Thrall Soby; Mr. Soichi Sunami; Mr. Justin K. Thannhauser; Mrs. G. David Thompson; Miss Jane Wade; Mrs. Florence Walters; Dr. Fernanda Wittgens

At the moment when this preface must go to the press certain important loans are still in doubt. Whether they are granted or not we should like to thank His Excellency, Georgi N. Zaroubin, Ambassador of the U.S.S.R., and Madame Tamara G. Mamedov, the Acting Cultural Attaché, for their efforts to secure the loan of ten paintings from the collections of the Hermitage Museum in Leningrad and the Pushkin Museum in Moscow; Dr. Juan Ainaud de Lasarte, Director of the Municipal Art Museums of Barcelona, for his part in negotiating loans from the Museo de Arte Moderno in Barcelona; and Mr. and Mrs. Joan Junyer for their generous, painstaking help in requesting loans from Don Sebastián Junyer Vidal of Barcelona.

I have also to thank my cooperative colleagues in the three museums associated as partners in the exhibition: Mr. Daniel Catton Rich, Director, Mrs. Katharine Kuh, Curator of Modern Painting and Sculpture, and Mr. Carl O. Schniewind, Curator of Prints and Drawings, all of The Art Institute of Chicago; Mr. Henri Marceau, Director, and Mr. Henry Clifford, Curator of Paintings, of The Philadelphia Museum of Art; Mr. René d'Harnoncourt, Director, Mr. Monroe Wheeler, Director of Exhibitions and Publications, and Mr. James Platt White, Special Assistant to the Director, of the Museum of Modern Art.

Mr. William S. Lieberman, Curator of Prints at the Museum of Modern Art, has not only organized the important drawing section of the exhibition but has been my right hand in many other ways; he has been ably assisted by the staff of the Print Room, Miss Dorothy L. Lytle, Assistant Curator, and Miss Edith Herman, Assistant. Mrs. E. Powis Jones has generously given many weeks of volunteer service in assembling photographs. My secretary, Miss Marie Alexander, with the help of Miss Betsy Jones, Secretary of the Museum Collections, have tirelessly borne the brunt of correspondence. Miss Dorothy C. Miller, Curator, and Miss Sara Mazo, Assistant Curator of the Museum Collections, have helped in installation; Miss Dorothy H. Dudley, Registrar, Miss Frances Pernas, Publications Manager, and Mrs. Elizabeth Shaw, Director of Publicity, indispensable pillars of all the Museum's exhibitions, have performed exceptionally arduous tasks in this one, as has the Museum's typographer, Mr. Charles Oscar. All have devoted to the exhibition, or its catalog, time and hard work far beyond their ordinary duties.

These thanks would be incomplete without acknowledging indebtedness to three publications which have proven indispensable in assembling and documenting the exhibition: the great catalogue by Christian Zervos which reproduces most of Picasso's work up through 1937; the catalogue of the grand Picasso retrospective presented in the Palazzo Reale, Milan, 1953; and the exemplary *catalogue raisonné* prepared by Maurice Jardot for the exhibition of Picasso's paintings presented under M. Jardot's direction at the Musée des Arts Décoratifs, Paris, in 1955.

This catalogue is simply a record of the exhibition. With it the Museum of Modern Art is publishing *Portrait of Picasso*, an admirable and richly illustrated documentation of Picasso's life by his friend, Roland Penrose. Among other books in English on Picasso now in print four general studies and one on his early period may be listed along with Mr. Penrose's work:

Roland Penrose, *Portrait of Picasso*, The Museum of Modern Art, New York, 1957
Frank Elgar and Robert Maillard, *Picasso*, Frederick A. Praeger, New York, 1956
Wilhelm Boeck and Jaime Sabartés, *Picasso*, Harry N. Abrams, New York, 1955
William S. Lieberman, *Picasso, Blue and Rose Periods*, Harry N. Abrams, with Pocket Books, New York, 1954
Maurice Raynal, *Picasso*, Skira, New York, 1953
Alfred H. Barr, Jr., *Picasso: Fifty Years of His Art*, The Museum of Modern Art, New York, 1946

Almost all of the works in this catalogue will be shown in both New York and Chicago. Most of them will also be shown in Philadelphia but for the exhibition opening in that city in January certain works will be replaced and revisions made in the catalogue.

ALFRED H. BARR, JR.
Director of the Exhibition

LENDERS TO THE EXHIBITION

Mr. Larry Aldrich, New York
Mr. and Mrs. Walter Bareiss, Greenwich, Connecticut
Mr. Ivan L. Best, Seattle
Mr. and Mrs. Leigh B. Block, Chicago
Mr. and Mrs. Harry Lynde Bradley, Milwaukee
Mr. Edward A. Bragaline, New York
Mr. and Mrs. William A. M. Burden, New York
Mrs. Meric Callery, New York
Mrs. Eleanor Rixson Cannon, New York
Mrs. Gilbert W. Chapman, New York
Mr. Stephen C. Clark, New York
Mr. and Mrs. Ralph F. Colin, New York
Madame Marie Cuttoli, Paris
Mr. and Mrs. Richard S. Davis, Wayzata, Minnesota
Mr. and Mrs. Richard Deutsch, Greenwich, Connecticut
Colonel Valdemar Ebbesen, Oslo
Mrs. Ingeborg Pudelko Eichmann, Florence
Mr. and Mrs. Victor W. Ganz, New York
Mr. and Mrs. Gerald Gidwitz, Highland Park, Illinois
Mr. Philip L. Goodwin, New York
Guennol Collection, New York
Mr. and Mrs. Ira Haupt, New York
Mr. Herbert Hemphill, Jr., New York
Mr. and Mrs. Alex L. Hillman, New York
Mr. Joseph H. Hirshhorn, New York
Miss Clara Hoover, New York
Mr. and Mrs. R. Sturgis Ingersoll, Penllyn, Pennsylvania
Mr. and Mrs. William B. Jaffe, New York
Mr. and Mrs. Sidney Janis, New York
Mr. Sebastián Junyer Vidal
Mr. Sylvester W. Labrot, Jr., Hobe Sound, Florida
Mr. André Lefèvre, Paris
Mrs. List-Israel, New York
Mrs. Gates Lloyd, Haverford, Pennsylvania
Mr. Henry P. McIlhenny, Philadelphia
Mlle Dora Maar, Paris
Mr. and Mrs. Arnold H. Maremont, Chicago
Florene and Samuel Marx, Chicago
Mr. and Mrs. Wilbur D. May, Reno
Mr. and Mrs. Morton G. Neumann, Chicago
Mr. Clifford Odets, Beverly Hills, California
Mrs. Culver Orswell, Pomfret Center, Connecticut
Mr. and Mrs. William S. Paley, New York
Mr. and Mrs. Roland Penrose, London
Mr. Pablo Picasso, Cannes
Louise and Joseph Pulitzer, Jr., St. Louis
Mr. Nelson A. Rockefeller, New York
Dr. and Mrs. Israel Rosen, Baltimore
Mr. Siegfried Rosengart, Lucerne
Herbert and Nannette Rothschild, New York
Mr. Jaime Sabartés, Paris
Mr. and Mrs. Daniel Saidenberg, New York
Mr. Georges A. Salles, Paris
Mr. Jacques Sarlie, New York
Mrs. Louise Smith, New York
Mr. and Mrs. James Thrall Soby, New Canaan, Connecticut

Women of Algiers. Final version, 14 February 1955. $44\frac{7}{8} \times 57\frac{1}{2}''$. Collection Mr. and Mrs. Victor W. Ganz, New York

Mr. and Mrs. Nate B. Spingold, New York
Mr. Louis E. Stern, New York
Mr. and Mrs. Justin K. Thannhauser, New York
Mr. G. David Thompson, Pittsburgh
Dr. Herschel Carey Walker, New York
Mr. and Mrs. John W. Warrington, Cincinnati
Ambassador and Mrs. John Hay Whitney, London
Mr. and Mrs. S. J. Zacks, Toronto
Mr. and Mrs. William Zeckendorf, Jr., New York
The Anonymous Lenders

Fine Arts Associates, New York
Galerie Louise Leiris, Paris
Perls Galleries, New York
Paul Rosenberg & Co., New York
The Saidenberg Gallery, New York
J. K. Thannhauser, New York

The Baltimore Museum of Art
Museo de Arte Moderno, Barcelona
The Kunstmuseum, Basle
The Albright Art Gallery, Buffalo
The Fogg Art Museum, Harvard University, Cambridge
The Art Institute of Chicago
The Wadsworth Atheneum, Hartford
Museo de Arte Moderno, Madrid
The Metropolitan Museum of Art, New York
The Museum of Modern Art, New York
The Allen Memorial Art Museum, Oberlin College
Nasjonalgalleriet, Oslo
Musée National d'Art Moderne, Paris
The Philadelphia Museum of Art
The Santa Barbara Museum of Art, California
The Toledo Museum of Art, Ohio

CATALOGUE AND PLATES

Self Portrait. (1901). Oil on canvas, 29 x 23¼". Private collection, New York

The arrangement is approximately chronological.

Whenever feasible the relative size of the reproductions within each double-page spread reflects approximately the relative size of the works themselves.

Because of lack of space or late arrival of photographs some works included in the exhibition could not be illustrated. References are given to reproductions of these works in other publications.

The place where the work was done and the date are given *without* parentheses if these data occur on the work itself and appear to be by the artist's hand. Data drawn from other sources are placed in parentheses.

Dimensions are given in inches; height precedes width.

Abbreviations:

"Zervos" refers to Christian Zervos, *Pablo Picasso*, Paris, Cahiers d'Art, 8 volumes, 1932-57.

"Picasso 50" refers to Alfred H. Barr, Jr., *Picasso: Fifty Years of His Art*, New York, Museum of Modern Art, 1946.

LEFT: *Gypsy Girl.* (1898?). Oil and pastel, 18½ x 24¼″. Private collection

BELOW LEFT: *Seated Woman.* (1899). Bronze, 5½″ high. Mrs. List-Israel, New York

BELOW RIGHT: *Redemption.* (1898?). Watercolor and conté crayon, 17¾ x 11½″. Mr. and Mrs. Justin K. Thannhauser, New York

Le Moulin de la Galette. (Paris, autumn 1900). Oil on canvas, 35¼ x 45¾". Mr. and Mrs. Justin K. Thannhauser, New York

Page of Studies (Heads and Figures). (Paris, 1900). Conté crayon, 5⅛ x 8¼". Ivan L. Best, Seattle

Woman in Blue. (1901?). Oil on canvas, 52⅝ x 39¾″. Museo de Arte Moderno, Madrid

Dwarf Dancer (*La Nana*). (Paris, 1901). Oil on canvas, 40⅛ x 23⅝". Museo de Arte Moderno, Barcelona

LEFT: *Self Portrait.* (1901). Oil on cardboard mounted on wood, 20¼ x 12½". Ambassador and Mrs. John Hay Whitney, London

Sebastián Junyer Vidal. (Barcelona) June 1903. Oil on canvas, 49⅝ x 36". Sebastián Junyer Vidal, Barcelona

ABOVE: *Blind Man's Meal.* (Barcelona, 1903). Oil on canvas, 37½ x 37¼". The Metropolitan Museum of Art, New York, gift of Mr. and Mrs. Ira Haupt

LEFT: *Brooding Woman.* (Paris, 1904). Watercolor, 10⅝ x 14½". The Museum of Modern Art, New York, gift of Mr. and Mrs. Werner E. Josten

OPPOSITE: *Boy with Pipe.* (Paris, 1905). Oil on canvas, 39⅜ x 32″. Ambassador and Mrs. John Hay Whitney, London

LEFT: *Woman Ironing.* (Paris, 1904). Oil on canvas, 46⅛ x 29⅛″. Mr. and Mrs. Justin K. Thannhauser, New York. (Shown only in New York)

Meditation. (Paris, 1904). Watercolor, 13¾ x 10⅛″. Mrs. Louise Smith, New York

Man's Mask. 1904? (inscribed on cast: 04-1905; cf. Zervos VI, no. 597). Bronze, 7¾″ high. The Baltimore Museum of Art, Cone Collection

LEFT: *Woman with Crow.* (Paris) 1904. Gouache and pastel, 25½ x 19½″. The Toledo Museum of Art, gift of Edward Drummond Libbey

RIGHT: *Study for "The Actor" with profiles of Fernande.* (Paris, winter, 1904-05). Pencil, 18½ x 12⅜″ (sight). Nelson A. Rockefeller, New York

LEFT: *Woman with Chignon* (*Head of the Acrobat's Wife*). (Paris) 1904. Gouache, 16⅞ x 12¼″. The Art Institute of Chicago, bequest of Kate L. Brewster

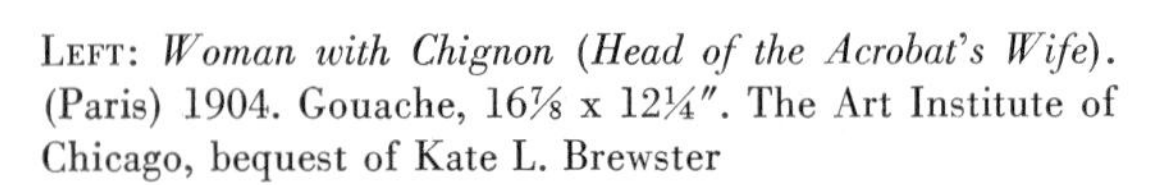

RIGHT: *Monkey.* (Paris, 1905). Watercolor and pen, 19¾ x 12⅝″. The Baltimore Museum of Art, Cone Collection

Circus Family. (Paris, 1905). Watercolor and pen, 9½ x 12″. The Baltimore Museum of Art, Cone Collection

ABOVE: *Two Acrobats with a Dog*. (Paris) 1905. Gouache on cardboard, 41½ x 29½″. Mr. and Mrs. William A. M. Burden, New York. (Shown in New York only)

LEFT: *Page of Studies* (*Figures and Bulls*). (Paris, 1905). Pen and ink, 12¾ x 9¾″. Nelson A. Rockefeller, New York

LEFT: *Head of a Man.* (1905?). Bronze 6½″ high. J. K. Thannhauser, New York
CENTER: *Head of a Woman* (1906). Bronze, 6¼″ high. Miss Clara Hoover, New York
RIGHT: *Head of a Girl.* (1906). Bronze, 4¾″ high. William Zeckendorf, Jr., New York

BELOW LEFT: *Head of a Jester.* (Paris, 1905). Bronze, 16¼″ high. Mrs. Louise Smith, New York
BELOW RIGHT: *Fernande.* 1905. Bronze, 14¼″ high. Allen Memorial Art Museum, Oberlin College, Ohio

:T: *Boy Leading a Horse.* (Paris, 1905). Oil
anvas, 87 x 51¼". Mr. and Mrs. William S.
y, New York

ow: *Boy on a Horse* (study for "The Water-
'lace"). (Paris, 1905). Charcoal, 18⅜ x 12".
and Mrs. John W. Warrington, Cincinnati

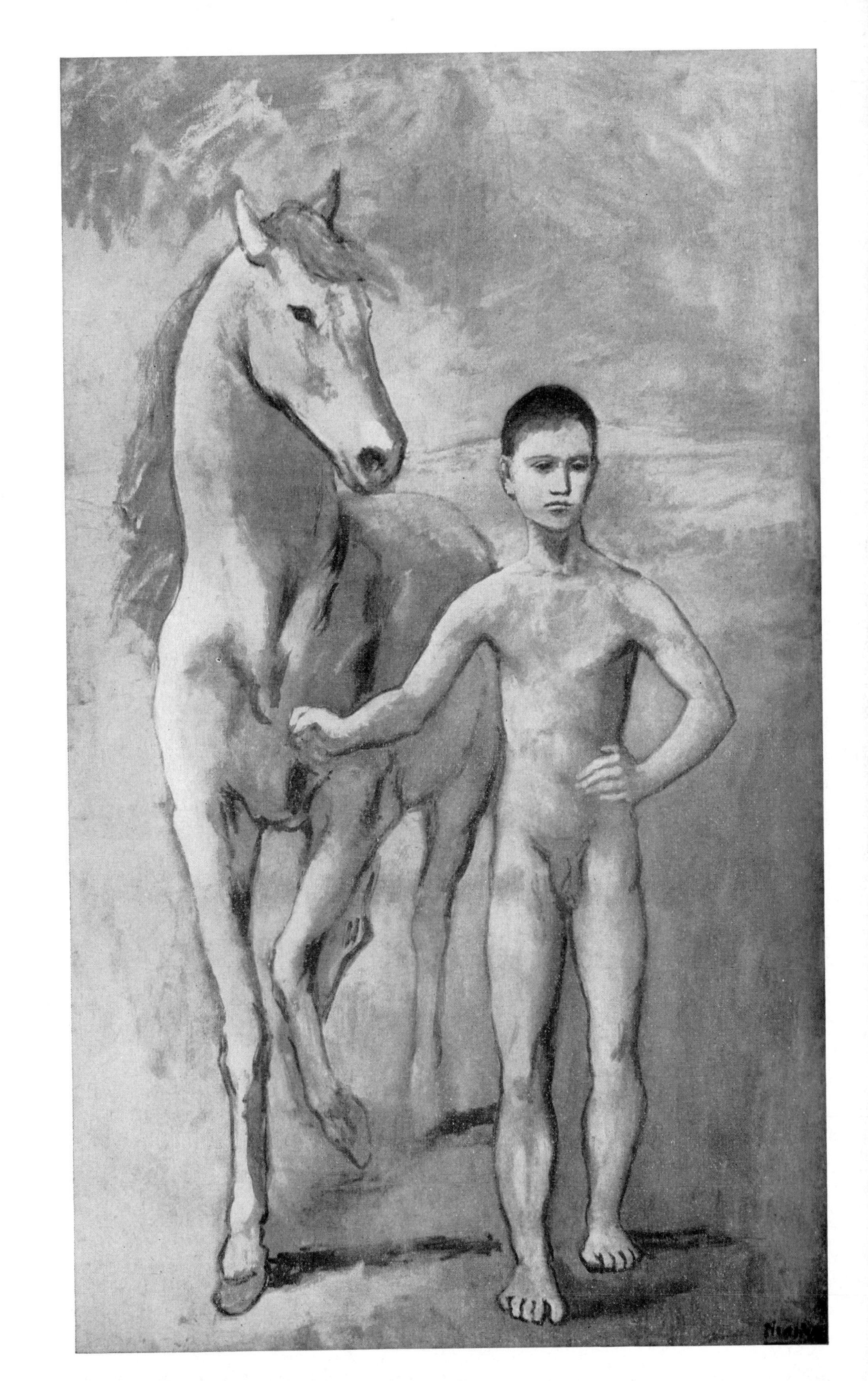

Landscape. (Gosol, summer 1906). Oil on canvas, 27½ x 39″. Mr. and Mrs. Nate B. Spingold, New York

LEFT: *The Blind Flower Vendor*. (1906). Ink and watercolor, 25 x 18¾″. Mr. and Mrs. S. J. Zacks, Toronto

RIGHT: *Peasants from Andorra*. (Gosol, summer 1906). Ink, 22⅝ x 13⅞″. The Art Institute of Chicago, gift of Robert Allerton

ABOVE LEFT: *Gertrude Stein.* (Paris, 1906). Oil on canvas, 39⅜ x 32″. The Metropolitan Museum of Art, New York, bequest of Gertrude Stein

ABOVE RIGHT: *Self Portrait.* (Paris, autumn) 1906. Oil on canvas, 36½ x 25¾″. Philadelphia Museum of Art, A. E. Gallatin Collection

LEFT: *Leo Stein.* (Paris, 1906). Gouache, 9¾ x 6¾″. The Baltimore Museum of Art, Cone Collection

LEFT: *Woman Combing her Hair.* (Paris, 1906). Oil on canvas, 49¾ x 35½". Florene and Samuel Marx, Chicago

BELOW: *Kneeling Woman Combing her Hair.* (1906). Bronze, 16⅝" high. Nelson A. Rockefeller, New York

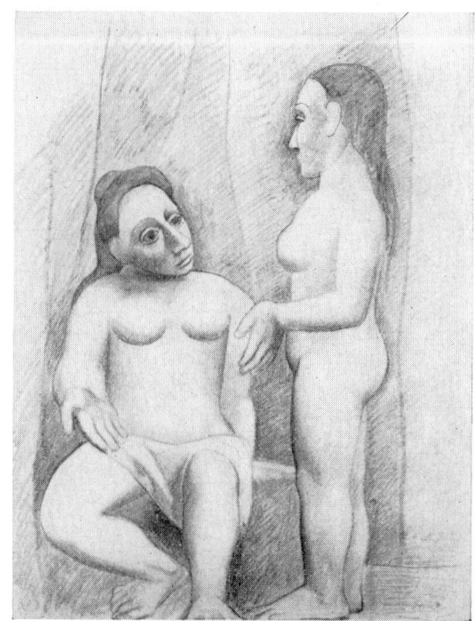

LEFT: *Two Women.* (Paris, late 1906). Charcoal, 24¾ x 18½". Mr. and Mrs. Richard S. Davis, Wayzata, Minnesota

RIGHT: *Woman Seated and Woman Standing.* (Paris, late 1906). Charcoal, 24⅛ x 18¼". Philadelphia Museum of Art, Louise and Walter Arensberg Collection

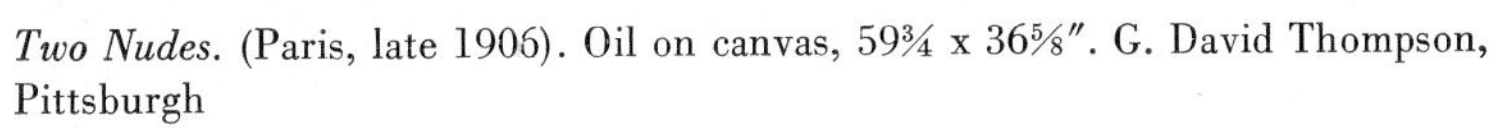

Two Nudes. (Paris, late 1906). Oil on canvas, 59¾ x 36⅝″. G. David Thompson, Pittsburgh

Two Nudes. (Paris, late 1906). Pencil and estompe, 24¾ x 18½″.
The Art Institute of Chicago, gift of Mrs. Potter Palmer

Above: *Harvesters.* (Paris, spring 1907). Oil on canvas, 25⅝ x 31⅞″. Nelson A. Rockefeller, New York

Below left: *Study for "Les Demoiselles d'Avignon."* (Paris, spring) 1907. Charcoal and pastel, 18⅞ x 25″. The artist

Below right: *Study for "Les Demoiselles d'Avignon."* (Paris, spring) 1907. Watercolor, 6¾ x 8¾″. Philadelphia Museum of Art, A. E. Gallatin Collection

Below: *Jug and Bowl.* (Paris, 1907; presented to Matisse 1907-08). Oil on wood, 24½ x 19″. Private collection, New York

Les Demoiselles d'Avignon. (Paris, spring 1907). Oil on canvas, 96 x 92″. The Museum of Modern Art, New York, acquired through the Lillie P. Bliss Bequest

Woman in Yellow. (Paris, summer 1907). Oil on canvas, 51¼ x 37⅜″. Louise and Joseph Pulitzer, Jr., St. Louis. (Shown in Chicago only)

Flowers. (Paris, summer 1907). Oil on canvas, 36½ x 28½″. Mr. and Mrs. Ralph F. Colin, New York

Seated Woman. (Paris, early 1908). Oil on canvas, 28¾ x 23½". Larry Aldrich, New York

Woman Sleeping. (Paris, spring 1908). Oil on canvas, 32 x 25½". André Lefèvre, Paris

LEFT: *Bathers in the Forest.* (Paris) 1908. Watercolor, 19⅛ x 23¾″. Mrs. Eleanor Rixson Cannon, New York

BELOW LEFT: *Kneeling Figure* (study for a figure composition). (Paris, 1908). Charcoal, 24⅝ x 18½″. Nelson A. Rockefeller, New York

BELOW RIGHT: *Head of a Woman.* (Paris, spring 1909). Black crayon and gouache, 24¼ x 18¾″. The Art Institute of Chicago, Charles L. Hutchinson Memorial (Edward E. Ayer Fund)

Woman with Pears. (Horta de San Juan, summer 1909). Oil on canvas, 36 x 28¾″. Florene and Samuel Marx, Chicago

Woman's Head. (1909). Bronze, 16¼″ high. The Museum of Modern Art, New York

LEFT: *Girl with Mandolin* (*Fanny Tellier*). (Paris, early) 1910. Oil on canvas, 39½ x 29". Nelson A. Rockefeller, New York

RIGHT: *Female Nude.* (Paris, late 1910). Oil on canvas, 38¾ x 30⅜". Philadelphia Museum of Art, Louise and Walter Arensberg Collection

OPPOSITE LEFT: *Female Nude.* (Paris, spring) 1910. Pen and ink watercolor, 29⅛ x 18⅜". Mr. and Mrs. Richard S. Davis, Way Minnesota

OPPOSITE RIGHT: *Nude.* (Paris, spring 1910). Charcoal, 19⅛ x 12¼". Metropolitan Museum of Art, New York, Alfred Stieglitz Collecti

Above left: *Wilhelm Uhde.* (Paris, spring 1910). Oil on canvas, 30¾ x 22¾". Roland Penrose, London

Above right: *D. H. Kahnweiler.* (Paris, autumn 1910). Oil on canvas, 39⅝ x 28⅝". The Art Institute of Chicago, gift of Mrs. Gilbert W. Chapman

BELOW LEFT: *Man with Pipe.* (Céret, summer 1911). Ink wash with charcoal, probably oil, 25 x 18¼″. Fogg Art Museum, Harvard University, Cambridge

BELOW CENTER: *Man with Pipe.* (1912). Charcoal, 24½ x 18½″. Dr. and Mrs. Israel Rosen, Baltimore

BELOW RIGHT: *Head of a Man.* (Paris, winter 1912-13). Charcoal, 24½ x 18⅝″. Private collection, New York

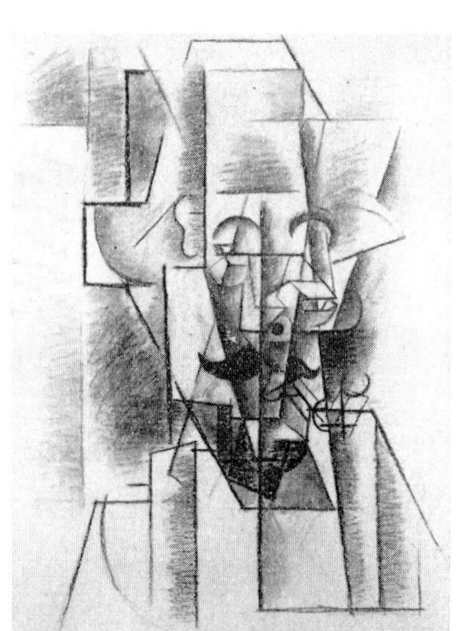

OPPOSITE PAGE

LEFT: *"Ma Jolie"* (woman with zither or guitar). (Paris, winter 1911-12). Oil on canvas, 39⅜ x 25¾″. The Museum of Modern Art, New York, acquired through the Lillie P. Bliss Bequest

RIGHT: *Man with Guitar*. Sorgues (summer) 1912 (completed in Paris, spring 1913). Oil on canvas, 51⅞ x 35″. Philadelphia Museum of Art, Louise and Walter Arensberg Collection

RIGHT: *Aficionado* (*Bullfight Fan*). Sorgues (summer) 1912. Oil on canvas, 53¼ x 32½″. Oeffentliche Kunstsammlung, Kunstmuseum, Basle

BELOW: *"Le Torero."* Céret (summer 1911). Oil on canvas, 18¼ x 15″. Nelson A. Rockefeller, New York

Still Life with Chair Caning. (Paris, winter 1911-12). Oil, pasted oilcloth simulating chair caning on canvas, 10⅝ x 13¾″ (oval). The artist

Below left: *Bottle of "Vieux Marc," Glass, Newspaper.* (Céret, spring 1912). Charcoal and pasted papers, 24⅝ x 18½″. Mme Marie Cuttoli, Paris

Below center: *Guitar.* (Spring 1912). Charcoal and pasted papers, 24½ x 18½″ (sight). Nelson A. Rockefeller, New York

Right: *Man with Violin.* (Paris, winter 1912-13). Charcoal and pasted papers, 48⅝ x 18⅛″. G. David Thompson, Pittsburgh

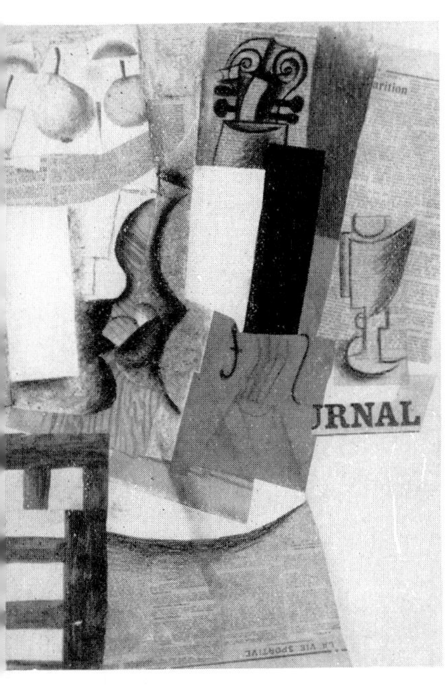

E LEFT: *Violin and Fruit.* (Paris, 1913). Charcoal and pasted papers, 25½ x 19½". Philadelphia Museum of Art, A. E. Gallatin Collection

E CENTER: *Still Life (Bottle and Glass).* (Paris, winter 1912-13). Charcoal, ink and pasted paper, 24⅞ x 18⅝". The Metropolitan Museum of Art, New , Alfred Stieglitz Collection

E RIGHT: *Head.* (Paris, 1914?). Charcoal and pasted papers on cardboard, 17⅛ x 13⅛". Roland Penrose, London

BELOW LEFT: *Still Life with Calling Card.* (Paris, 1914). Pencil and pasted papers, 5½ x 8¼". Mrs. Gilbert W. Chapman, New York

BELOW RIGHT: *Pipe, Glass, Bottle of Rum.* (Paris, 1914). Pencil, gouache and pasted papers on cardboard, 15¾ x 20¾". The Museum of Modern Art, New York, gift of Mr. and Mrs. Daniel Saidenberg

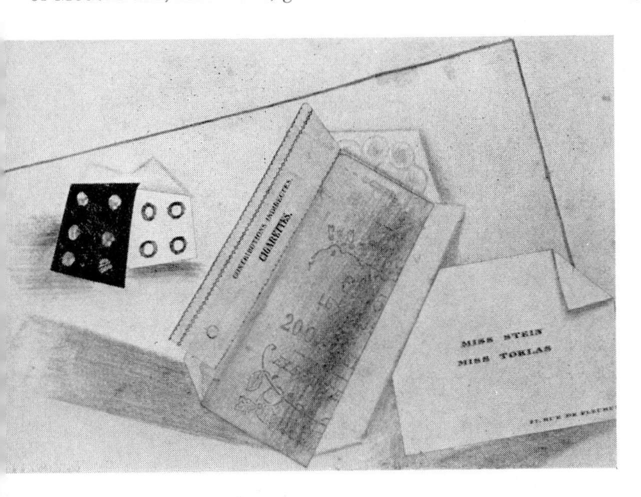

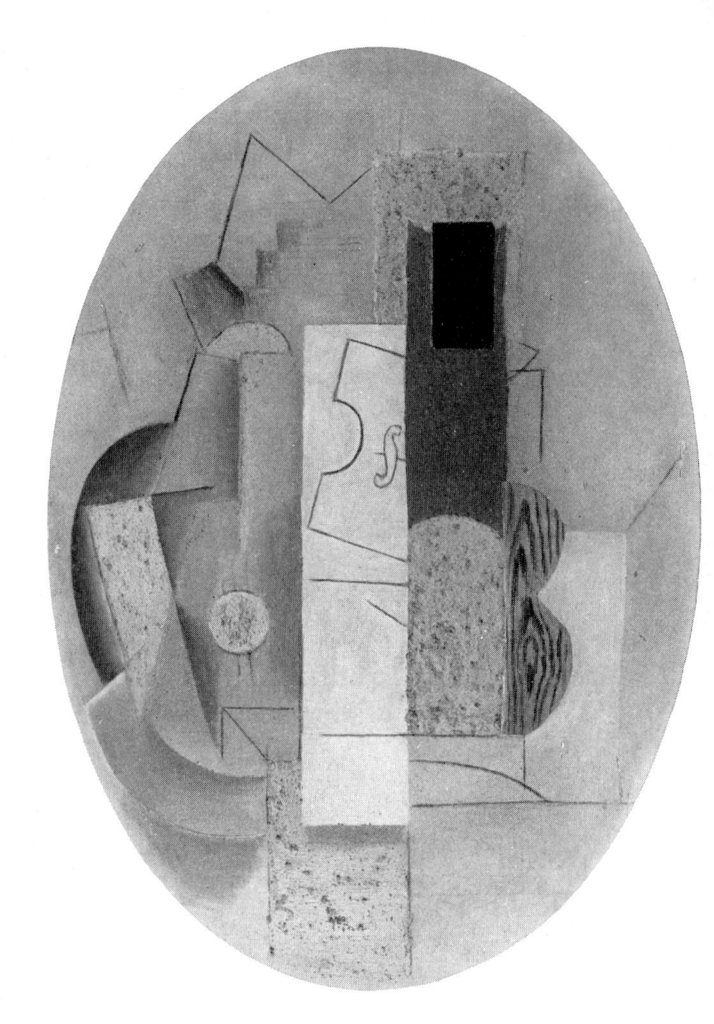

ABOVE: *Violin and Guitar*. (Paris, early) 1913. Pasted cloth, oil, pencil and plaster on canvas, 36 x 25″ (oval). Philadelphia Museum of Art, Louise and Walter Arensberg Collection

LEFT: *Guitar*. Sorgues (summer 1912). Oil on canvas, 28½ x 23⅝″ (oval). Nasjonalgalleriet, Oslo

Man with Hat. (Paris, December 1912). Charcoal, ink and pasted papers, 24½ x 18⅝″. (Reproduced Zervos II, no. 398 and Picasso 50, p. 80). The Museum of Modern Art, New York

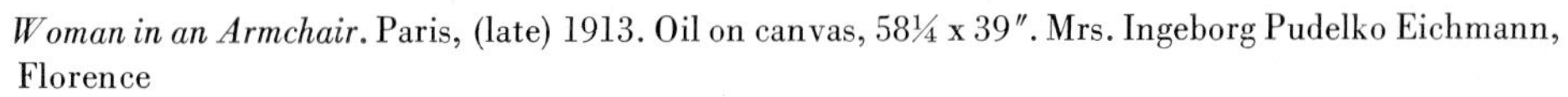

Woman in an Armchair. Paris, (late) 1913. Oil on canvas, 58¼ x 39″. Mrs. Ingeborg Pudelko Eichmann, Florence

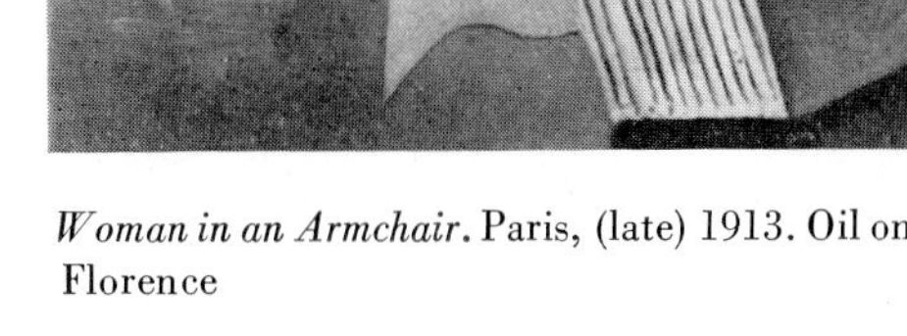

LEFT: *Bird.* (Late 1913). Oil on canvas, 13 x 5⅞″. Private collection, New York

ABOVE: *Glass of Absinth.* (1914). Painted bronze and silver spoon, 7⅛″ high. The Museum of Modern Art, New York, gift of Mrs. Louise Smith

LEFT: *Portrait of a Girl.* Avignon, 1914. Oil on canvas, 51¼ x 38⅛″. Georges A. Salles, Paris

BELOW: *Still Life.* (1914). Painted wood with upholstery fringe, 18⅞″ long. Roland Penrose, London

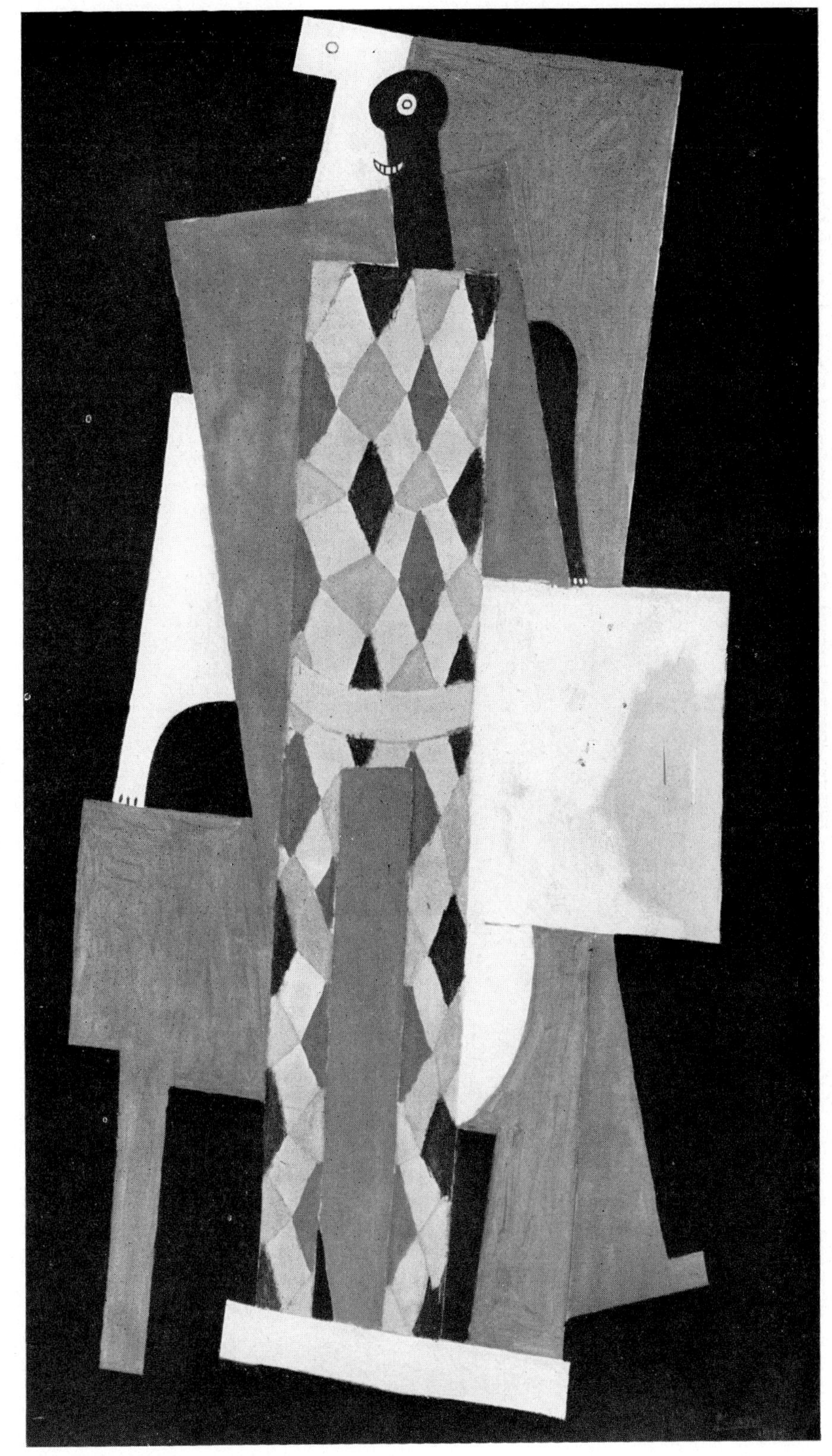

Harlequin. (Paris, late) 1915. Oil on canvas, 72¼ x 41⅜″. The Museum of Modern Art, New York, acquired through the Lillie P. Bliss Bequest

BELOW: *Head of a Young Man.* (Paris). 1915. Oil on wood, 10 x 7¼″. Fine Arts Associates, New York

LEFT: *Ambroise Vollard.* Paris, August 1915. Pencil, 18⅜ x 12½. The Metropolitan Museum of Art, New York, Whittelsey Fund

BELOW LEFT: *Diaghilev and Selisburg.* (1919). Pencil, 24⅞ x 18⅞". The artist

BELOW RIGHT: *Three Ballerinas.* (Paris, 1919). Pencil and charcoal, 23⅛ x 17⅜". The artist

Sleeping Peasants. (Paris) 1919. Gouache, 12¼ x 19¼″. The Museum of Modern Art, New York, Mrs. John D. Rockefeller, Jr. Fund

BELOW LEFT: *Two Peasants* (*Bride and Groom*). (Paris) 1919. Conté crayon 23½ x 18¼″. Santa Barbara Museum of Art, gift of Wright Ludington

BELOW RIGHT: *Fisherman.* (Biarritz?) 1918. Pencil, 13¾ x 10″ (sight). Private collection, New York

LEFT: *Bathers.* (Biarritz) 1918. Pencil, 9⅛ x 12¼″. Fogg Art Museum, Harvard University, Cambridge, Meta and Paul J. Sachs Collection

BELOW LEFT: *Page of Sketches.* (1919). Pencil, 12½ x 8⅝″. Mrs. Culver Orswell, Pomfret Center, Connecticut

BELOW CENTER: *Pierrot and Harlequin.* (Paris) 1918. Pencil, 10¼ x 7½″. The Art Institute of Chicago, given in memory of Charles B. Goodspeed by Mrs. Gilbert W. Chapman

BELOW RIGHT: *Pierrot and Harlequin.* (Juan-les-Pins, summer 1920). Gouache, 10⅛ x 7¾″. Mrs. Gilbert W. Chapman, New York

TOP: *Nessus and Dejanira.* (Juan-les-Pins) 12 September 1920. Pencil, 8¼ x 10¼″. The Museum of Modern Art, New York, acquired through the Lillie P. Bliss Bequest

CENTER: *Nessus and Dejanira.* (Juan-les-Pins) 22 September 1920. Silverpoint, 8¾ x 10⅝″. Nelson A. Rockefeller, New York

BELOW RIGHT: *Nessus and Dejanira with a Satyr.* (Juan-les-Pins) 12 September 1920. Watercolor, 8½ x 11¼″. Private collection, New York

BELOW LEFT: *Two Ballet Dancers.* (London, summer 1919). Pencil, 12¼ x 9¼″. Mr. and Mrs. Victor W. Ganz, New York

Study of a Hand. (Paris) 20 January 1921. Pastel, 8⅛ x 12½″. (Reproduced Zervos IV, no. 239 and Picasso 50, p. 119). Nelson A. Rockefeller, New York

Three Musicians. (Fontainebleau, summer) 1921. Oil on canvas, 80 x 74″. Philadelphia Museum of Art, A. E. Gallatin Collection

Three Musicians. Fontainebleau (summer) 1921. Oil on canvas, 79 x 87¾″. The Museum of Modern Art, New York, Mrs. Simon Guggenheim Fund

Above left: *Dr. Claribel Cone.* 14 July 1922. Pencil, 24¾ x 19¼". The Baltimore Museum of Art, Cone Collection

Above right: *St. Servan, near Dinard.* (1922). Pencil, 16⅛ x 11⅛" (Sight). Mr. and Mrs. Justin K. Thannhauser, New York

Right: *Standing Nude.* 1922. Oil on canvas, 10¼ x 8½". Private collection, New York

LEFT, ABOVE: *Four Bathers.* 1921. Tempera on wood, 4 x 6″. Private collection, New York

LEFT, BELOW: *The Rape,* 1920. Tempera on wood, 9⅜ x 12⅞″. Philip L. Goodwin, New York

BELOW LEFT: *Standing Nude.* (Dinard) 1922. Oil on wood, 7½ x 5½″. Wadsworth Atheneum, Hartford

BELOW CENTER: *Nude Seated on a Rock.* (1921). Tempera on wood, 5⅞ x 3⅞″. Mr. and Mrs. James Thrall Soby, New Canaan, Conn.

BELOW RIGHT: *Actor in Green.* 1922. Gouache on paper, 6⅜ x 4½″. Stephen C. Clark, New York

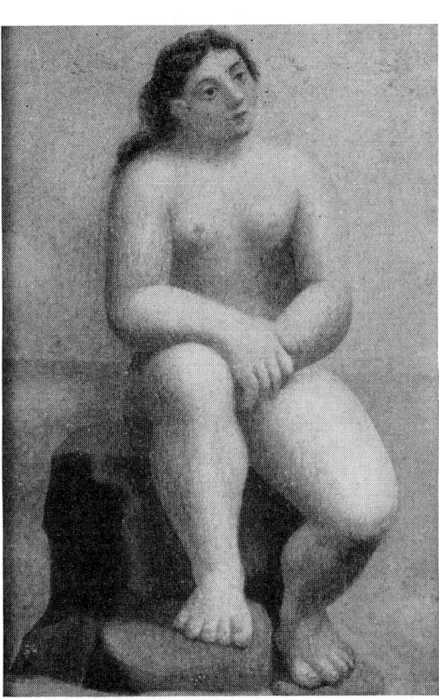

By the Sea. (Juan-les-Pins, summer 1920) dated by error "1923." Oil on wood, 32 x 39½". G. David Thompson, Pittsburgh

The Race. (Paris, 1922). Tempera on wood, 12⅞ x 16¼". The artist

Mother and Child. 1921. Oil on canvas, 56½ x 64″. The Art Institute of Chicago

LEFT: *Mandolin on a Table.* (Paris) 1922. Oil on canvas, 31⅞ x 39⅝". Mr. and Mrs. William B. Jaffe, New York

BELOW: *The Red Tablecloth.* (Paris, December) 1924. Oil on canvas, 38¾ x 51⅜". Private collection, New York

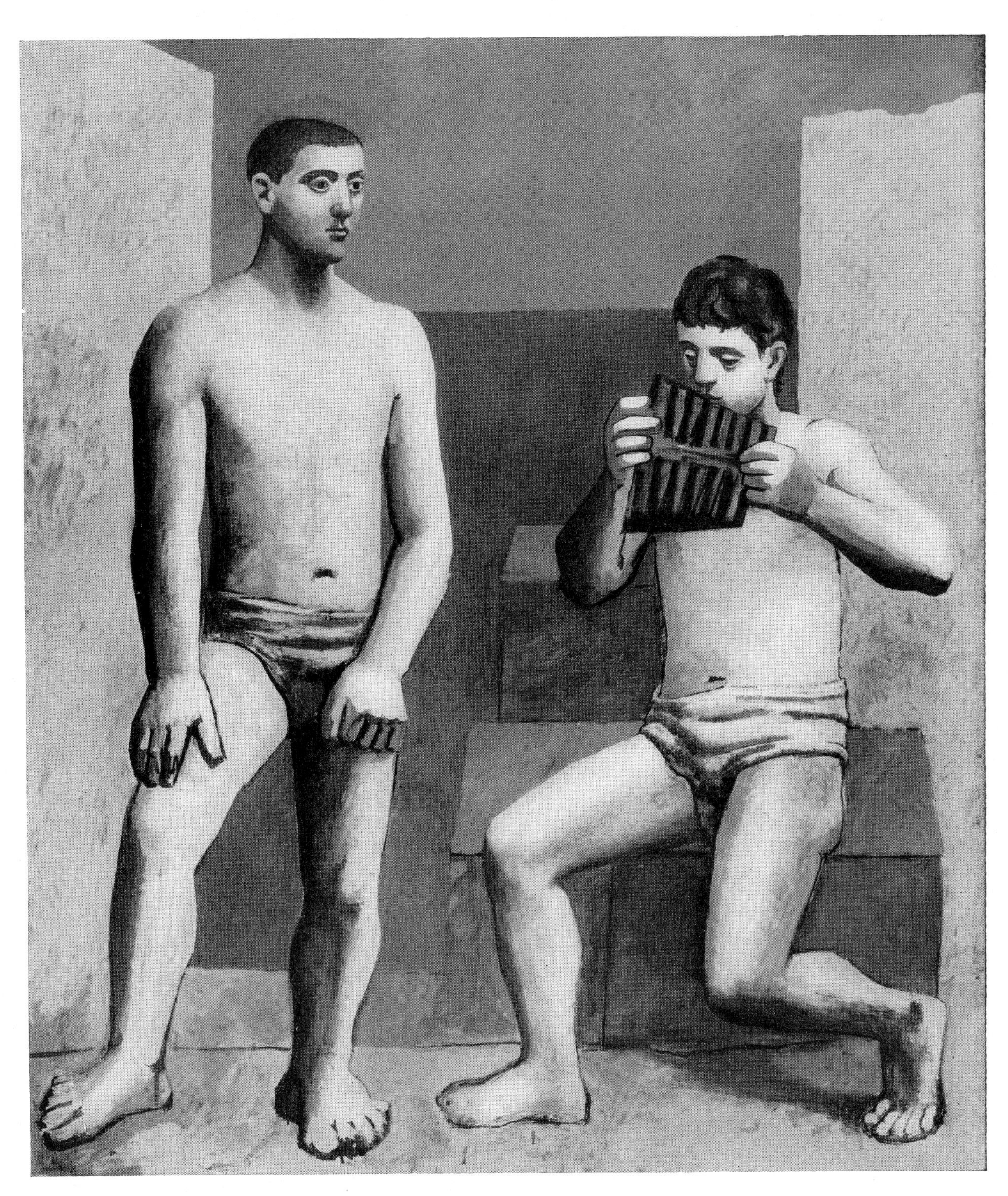

The Pipes of Pan. (1923). Oil on canvas, 80½ x 68⅝". The artist

Paul as Harlequin. 1924. Oil on canvas, 51⅛ x 38⅛″. The artist

Paul as Pierrot. (February) 1925. Oil on canvas, 51⅛ x 38⅛″. The artist

RIGHT: *Harlequin with Guitar*. 1924. Oil on canvas, 51¼ x 38¼″. Mr. and Mrs. Leigh B. Block, Chicago

BELOW: *Ram's Head*. (Juan-les-Pins, summer) 1925. Oil on canvas, 32⅛ x 39½″. Private collection, New York

Three Dancers. (1925). Oil on canvas, 84⅝ x 56¼″. The artist

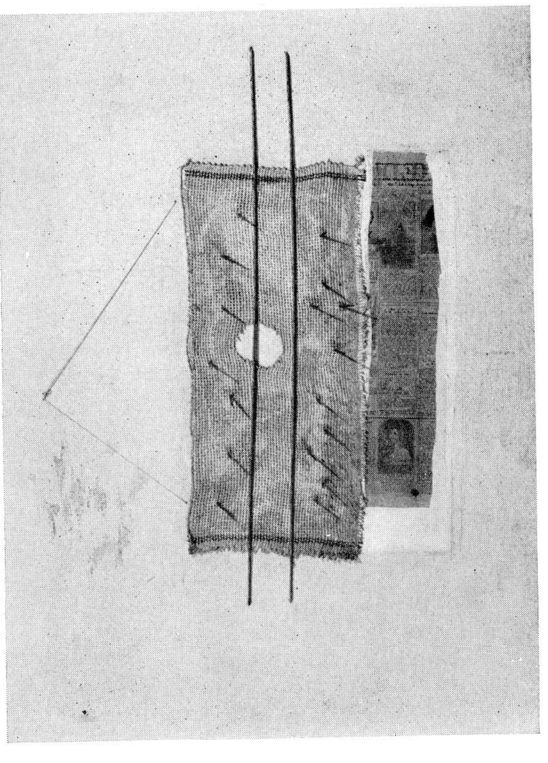

Above: *Running Monster*. April 1928. Oil on canvas, 63¾ x 51¼". The artist

Above left: *Head*. (1927). Oil and plaster on canvas, 39¼ x 31¾". The Art Institute of Chicago, gift of Mr. and Mrs. Samuel A. Marx

Below left: *Guitar* (1926). Canvas with string, pasted paper, oil paint and cloth with two inch nails, points out, 51¼ x 38¼". The artist

Seated Woman. 1927. Oil on wood, 51⅛ x 38¼". Mr. and Mrs James Thrall Soby, New Canaan

Figure. (1927). Oil on wood, 51⅛ x 38⅛". The artist

ABOVE: *Painter and Model.* 1928. Oil on canvas, 51⅝ x 63⅞". Mr. and Mrs. Sidney Janis, New York

LEFT: *Bather and Cabin.* (Dinard, 9 August) 1928. Oil on canvas, 8½ x 6¼". The Museum of Modern Art, New York, Hillman Periodicals Fund

LEFT: *Seated Bather*. (Early 1930). Oil on canvas, 64¼ x 51″. The Museum of Modern Art, New York, Mrs. Simon Guggenheim Fund
RIGHT: *Figure by the Sea*. (7 April) 1929. Oil on canvas, 51 x 38″. Florene and Samuel Marx, Chicago

Pitcher and Bowl of Fruit. (Paris) 22 February 1931. Oil on canvas, 51½ x 63″. Nelson A. Rockefeller, New York

Crucifixion. (Paris) 7 February 1930. Oil on wood, 20 x 26″. The artist

Woman in an Armchair. 5 May 1929. Oil on canvas, 76¾ x 51⅛″. The artist

Still Life on a Table. 11 March 1931. Oil on canvas, 76¾ x 51⅝″. The artist

Bather Playing Ball. Boisgeloup, 30 August 1932. Oil on canvas, 57½ x 45″. The artist

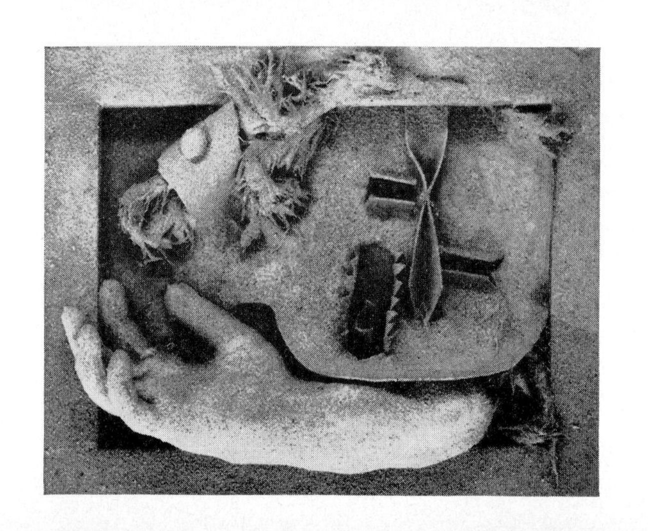

TOP: *Design for sculpture.* (1932). Crayon on canvas, 36⅜ x 28¾. G. David Thompson, Pittsburgh

CENTER: *Sculptor and his Statue.* Cannes, 20 July 1933. Gouache and ink, 15⅜ x 19⅜" (sight). Private Collection, New York

BOTTOM: *By the Sea.* (Juan-les-Pins) 22 August 1930. Sand over cardboard, plaster and canvas, 10⅝ x 13¾". The artist

BELOW RIGHT: *Cock.* (1932). Bronze, 25½" high, Mr. and Mrs. William A. M. Burden, New York

Girl before a Mirror. (Paris) 14 March 1932. Oil on canvas, 63¾ x 51¼″. The Museum of Modern Art, New York, gift of Mrs. Simon Guggenheim

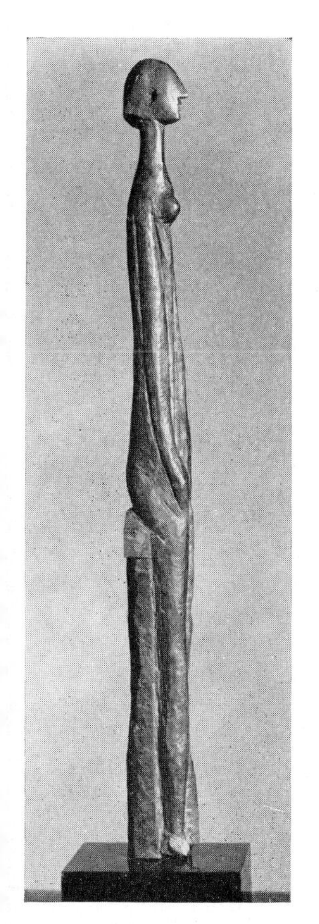

Standing Woman. (1931). Bronze after carved wood, 21½″ high. Mrs. Meric Callery, New York

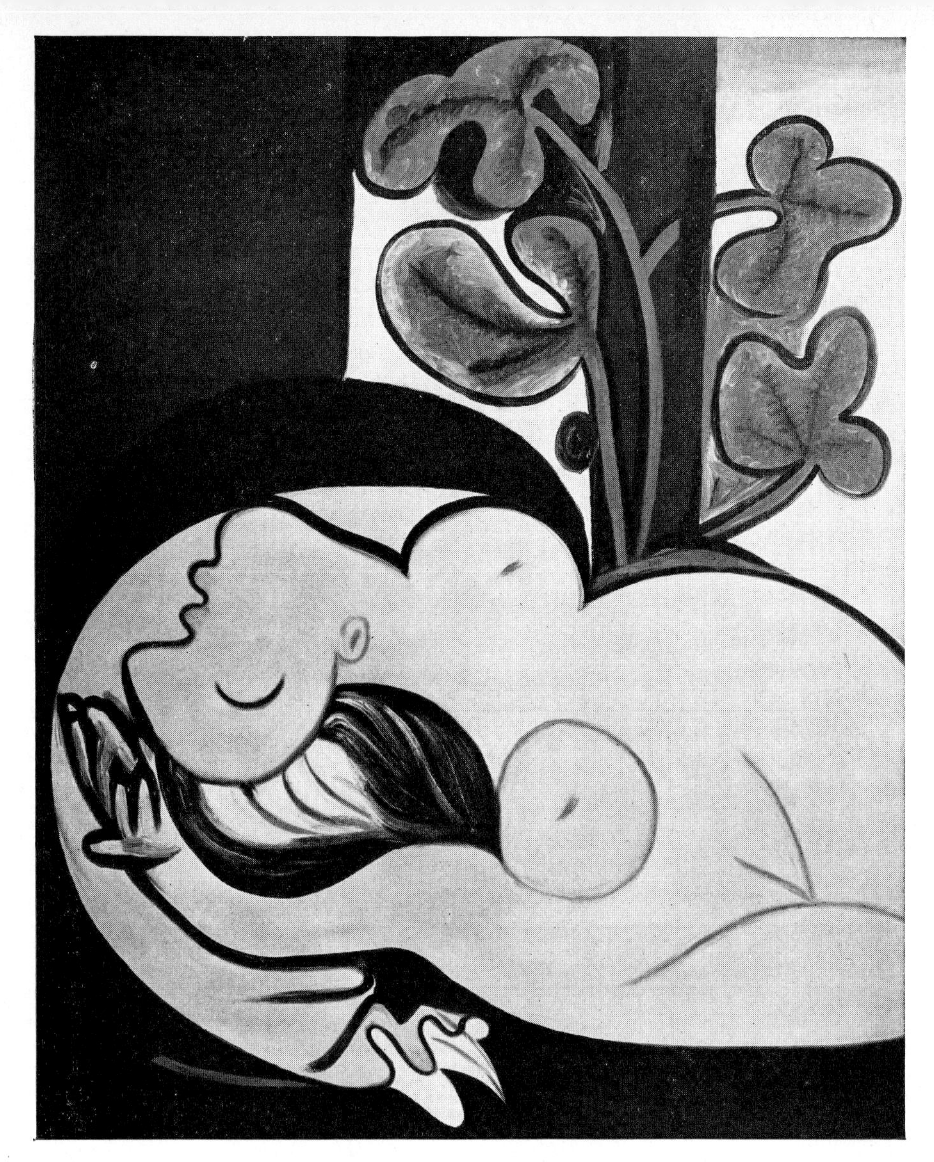

Nude on a Black Couch. (Paris) 9 March 1932. Oil on canvas, 63¾ x 51¼". Mrs. Meric Callery, New York

The Balcony. Cannes, 1 August 1933. Watercolor and ink, 15¾ x 19⅞". Mrs. Louise Smith, New York

FT: *Man Ray*. Paris, 3 January 1934. Pen and ink ısh, 13⅝ x 9¾″. Clifford Odets, Beverly Hills

GHT: "*Minotaure*" (design for a magazine cover). 933). Pencil drawing with pasted papers and cloth cked on wood, 19⅛ x 16⅛″. Private collection, New ɔrk

udy for illustrations to "Lysistrata." Paris, 11 January 34. Brush and ink, 14¼ x 19⅞″ (Reproduced ɜrvos VIII, no. 160). Mrs. Meric Callery, New York

EFT: *The Minotaur*. Boisgeloup, 24 June 1933. Pen and ink wash, 18⅞ x 24¾″. Sylvester W. Labrot, Jr., Hobe Sound, Florida

GHT: *Bullfight*. Boisgeloup, 9 September 1934. Oil on canvas, 13 x 16⅛″. Henry P. McIlhenny, Philadelphia

LEFT: *Woman with Hat.* (Paris, 1935). Oil on canvas, 30 x 24½″. Georges A. Salles, Paris

CENTER: *Harlequin* (project for a monument). Paris, 10 March 1935. Oil on canvas, 24¼ x 20″. Room of Contemporary Art Collection, Albright Art Gallery, Buffalo

RIGHT: *Portrait of D. M.* (Paris) 19 November 1936, Oil on canvas, 25¼ x 21¼″. Mme Marie Cuttoli, Paris

BELOW: *Reclining Nude.* (Paris) 12 August—2 October 1936. Oil on canvas, 51¼ x 63¾″. Private collection, Paris

GUERNICA—1937
20th Anniversary—1957

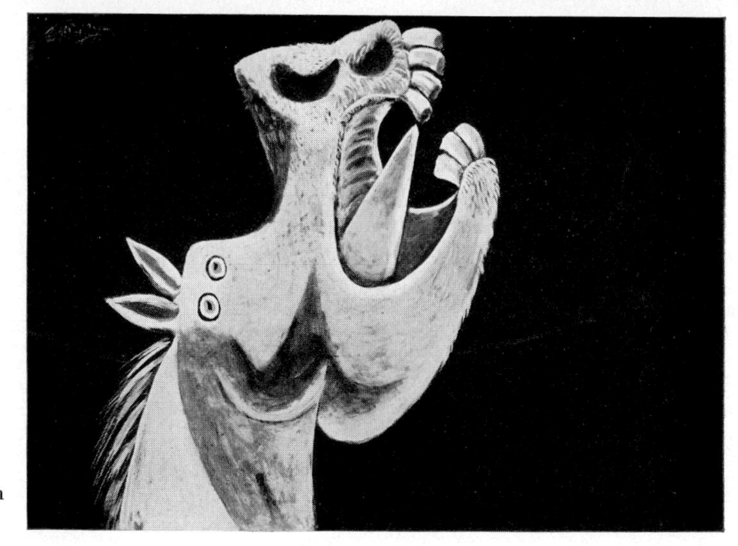

Horse's Head. May 2, 1937. Oil on canvas. 25½ x 36¼″. The artist

Guernica, the ancient capital of the Basque people in northern Spain, was largely destroyed on April 27th, 1937 by German bombers flying for General Franco. It was the first "saturation" bombing of a city in military history.

Some months earlier Picasso had been commissioned to paint a mural in the Spanish Republic building at the Paris World's Fair. He had done nothing about it until the news of the Guernica catastrophe aroused him to a fury of action. On May 1st he made the first sketches; on May 10 he began to paint; in June the mural was installed.

There have been many and often contradictory interpretations of the *Guernica*. Picasso himself has denied it any political significance stating simply that the mural expresses his abhorrence of war and brutality

The *Guernica* and the studies and "postscripts" listed below are lent by the artist. Almost all are reproduced in *Guernica* by Juan Larrea, New York, Curt Valentin, 1947.

Guernica studies and "postscripts"

1 May 1937

Three *Composition studies*. Pencil on blue paper, each 8¼ x 10⅝″.

Two *Studies for the horse*. Pencil on blue paper, each 8¼ x 10½″.

Composition study. Pencil on gesso on wood, 21⅛ x 25½″.

2 May 1937

Composition study. Pencil on gesso on wood, 23⅝ x 28¾″.

Two *Studies for horse's head*. Pencil on blue paper, 8¼x 6″ and 10½ x 8¼″

Horse's head. Oil on canvas, 25½ x 36¼″

(Early May 1937?)

Horse and bull. Pencil on tan paper, 8⅞ x 4¾″

continued on page 78

Left: Composition study for *Guernica*. May 1, 1937. Pencil on blue paper, 8¼ x 10⅝″. The artist

Right: Composition study for *Guernica*. May 9, 1937. Pencil on white paper, 9½ x 17⅞″. The artist

Guernica. (Paris, May—early June 1937). Oil on canvas, 11′5½″ x 25′5¾″. Extended loan by the artist to the Museum of Modern Art, New York

8 May 1937

Composition study. Pencil on white paper, 9½ x 17⅞″

Horse and mother with dead child. Pencil on white paper, 9½ x 17⅞″

9 May 1937

Mother with dead child. Ink on white paper, 9½ x 17⅞″

Composition study. Pencil on white paper, 9½ x 17⅞″

Mother with dead child on ladder. Pencil on white paper, 17⅞ x 9½″

10 May 1937

Study for the horse. Pencil on white paper, 9½ x 17⅞″

Studies for the horse. Pencil on white paper, 17⅞ x 9½″

Bull's head with human face. Pencil on white paper, 17⅞ x 9½″

Study for the horse. Pencil and color crayon on white paper, 9½ x 17⅞″

Mother with dead child on ladder. Color crayon and pencil on white paper, 17⅞ x 9½″

11 May 1937

Bull with human face. Pencil on white paper, 9½ x 17⅞″

13 May 1937

Woman's head. Pencil and color crayon on white paper, 17⅞ x 9½″

Hand with broken sword. Pencil on white paper, 9½ x 17⅞″

Mother with dead child. Color crayon and pencil on white paper, 9½ x 17⅞″

20 May 1937

Horse's head. Pencil and wash on white paper, 11½ x 9¼″

Horse's head. Pencil and wash on white paper, 9¼ x 11½″

Two *Studies for bull's head.* Pencil and wash on white paper, each 9¼ x 11½″

Woman's head. Pencil and wash on white paper, 11½ x 9¼″

24 May 1937

Two *Studies for weeping head.* Pencil and wash on white paper, each 11½ x 9¼″

Head. Pencil and wash on white paper, 9¼ x 11½″

27 May 1937

Weeping head. Pencil and wash on white paper, 9¼ x 11½″

Falling man. Pencil and wash on white paper, 9¼ x 11½″

28 May 1937

Mother with dead child. Pencil, color crayon, gouache and hair on white paper, 9¼ x 11½″

Mother with dead child. Pencil, color crayon and gouache on white paper, 9¼ x 11½″

Weeping head. Pencil, color crayon and gouache on white paper, 9¼ x 11½″

31 May 1937

Weeping head. Pencil, color crayon and gouache on white paper, 9¼ x 11½″

3 June 1937

Three *Studies for a weeping head.* Pencil, color crayon and gouache on white paper, each 9¼ x 11½″

Head and horse's hoofs. Pencil and wash on white paper, 9¼ x 11½″

4 June 1937

Study for man's head. Pencil and wash on white paper, 9¼ x 11½″

Study for hand. Pencil and wash on white paper, 9¼ x 11½″

8 June 1937

Weeping head. Pencil, color crayon and wash on white paper, 11½ x 9¼″

Weeping head. Pencil and wash on white paper, 11½ x 9¼″

13 June 1937

Weeping head. Pencil and color crayon on white paper, 11½ x 9¼″

15 June 1937

Weeping head. Pencil, color crayon and oil on canvas, 21⅝ x 18⅛″

Weeping head. Pencil and gouache on cardboard, 4⅝ x 3½″

22 June 1937

Weeping head with handkerchief. Oil on canvas, 21⅝ x 18⅛″

Mother with dead child. Pencil, color crayon and oil on canvas, 21⅝ x 18⅛″

(4) July 1937

Weeping head with handkerchief. Ink on white paper, 10 x 6¾″

6 July 1937

Weeping head with handkerchief. Ink on tan paper, 6 x 4½″

26 September 1937

Mother with dead child. Oil on canvas, 51¼ x 76¾″

12 October 1937

Weeping head. Ink and pencil on white paper, 35⅜ x 23″

13 October 1937

Weeping head with handkerchief. Ink and oil on canvas, 21⅝ x 18⅛″

17 October 1937

Weeping woman with handkerchief. Oil on canvas, 36¼ x 28⅝″

Above: *Weeping Woman.* (Paris) 26 October 1937. Oil on canvas, 23½ x 19¼". Roland Penrose, London

Right: *Girl with Cock.* (Paris) 15 February 1938. Oil on canvas, 57¼ x 47½". Mrs. Meric Callery, New York

LEFT: *Man with Lollipop.* (Mougins) 20 August 1938. Oil on paper on canvas, 26⅞ x 18″. Edward A. Bragaline, New York

RIGHT: *Cock.* (Paris) 29 March 1938. Pastel, 30½ x 21¼″. Mr. and Mrs. Ralph F. Colin, New York

BELOW LEFT: *Still Life.* (Paris) 4 February 1939. Oil on canvas, 13 x 18″. Dr. Herschel Carey Walker, New York

BELOW RIGHT: *Three Women.* (Mougins) 10 August 1938. Pen and ink wash, 17½ x 26⅝″. Mrs. Meric Callery, New York

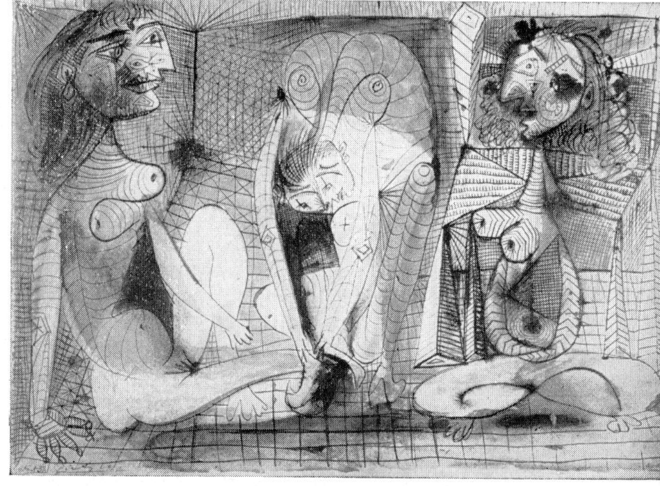

Still Life with Black Bull's Head. (Paris) 19 November 1938. Oil on canvas, 38¼ x 51¼″. Colonel Valdemar Ebbesen, Oslo

Still Life with Red Bull's Head. (Paris) 26 November 1938. Oil on canvas, 37¾ x 51″. Mr. and Mrs. William A. M. Burden, New York

LEFT: *Jaime Sabartés.* Royan, 22 October 1939. Oil on canvas, 23¾ x 18″. Jaime Sabartés, Paris
RIGHT: *Portrait of D. M.* (Paris) 1 April 1939. Oil, 36 x 28″. Mlle Dora Maar, Paris

BELOW LEFT: *Maïa with a Sailor Doll.* (Paris) 16 January 1938. Oil on canvas, 28¾ x 23⅝″. The artist
BELOW RIGHT: *Portrait of D. M.* (Royan) 30 December 1939. Gouache, 18⅛ x 15″. André Lefèvre, Paris

ght Fishing at Antibes. (August 1939). Oil on canvas, 6′9″ x 11′4″. The Museum of Modern Art, New York, Mrs. Simon Guggenheim Fund

LEFT: *Woman Dressing her Hair*. (Royan) 6 March 1940 (dated on stretcher, but possibly early June 1940). Oil on canvas, 51¼ x 38⅛". The artist

BELOW: *Still Life with Sausage*. (Paris) 10 May 1941. Oil on canvas, 35 x 25½". Mr. and Mrs. Victor W. Ganz, New York

enade (*L'Aubade*). (Paris) 4 May 1942. Oil on canvas, 6′4¾″ x 8′8¼″. Musée National d'Art Moderne, Paris

Portrait of D. M. (Paris) 9 October 1942. Oil on canvas, 36¼ x 28¾″. Mlle Dora Maar, Paris

Woman in Gray. (Paris) 6 August 1942. Oil on canvas, 39¼ x 31⅞″. Mr. and Mrs. Alex L. Hillman, New York

Woman in Green. 1943. Oil on canvas, 51 x 38″. Private collection, New York

The Striped Bodice. (Paris) 20 September 1943. Oil on canvas, 40 x 32½″. Nelson A. Rockefeller, New York

First Steps. (Paris) 21 May 1943. Oil on canvas, 51¼ x 38¼″. Stephen C. Clark, New York

Man with a Lamb. (Paris) 1944. Bronze, 7′4″ high.
Mr. and Mrs. R. Sturgis Ingersoll, Penllyn, Pa.

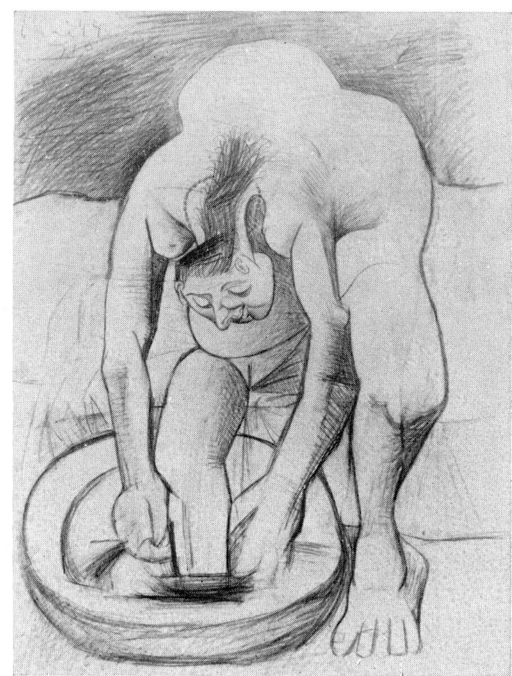

LEFT: *Woman Washing her Feet.* (Paris) 10 July 1944. Brush and ink, 20 x 13¼″. The Museum of Modern Art, New York

CENTER: *Woman Washing her Feet.* (Paris) 6 May 1944. Pencil, 19⅞ x 15⅛″. The Art Institute of Chicago, bequest of Curt Valentin

RIGHT: *Young Boy.* Paris, 13-15 August 1944. Ink and wash, 19½ x 11⅛″ (sight). Florene and Samuel Marx, Chicago

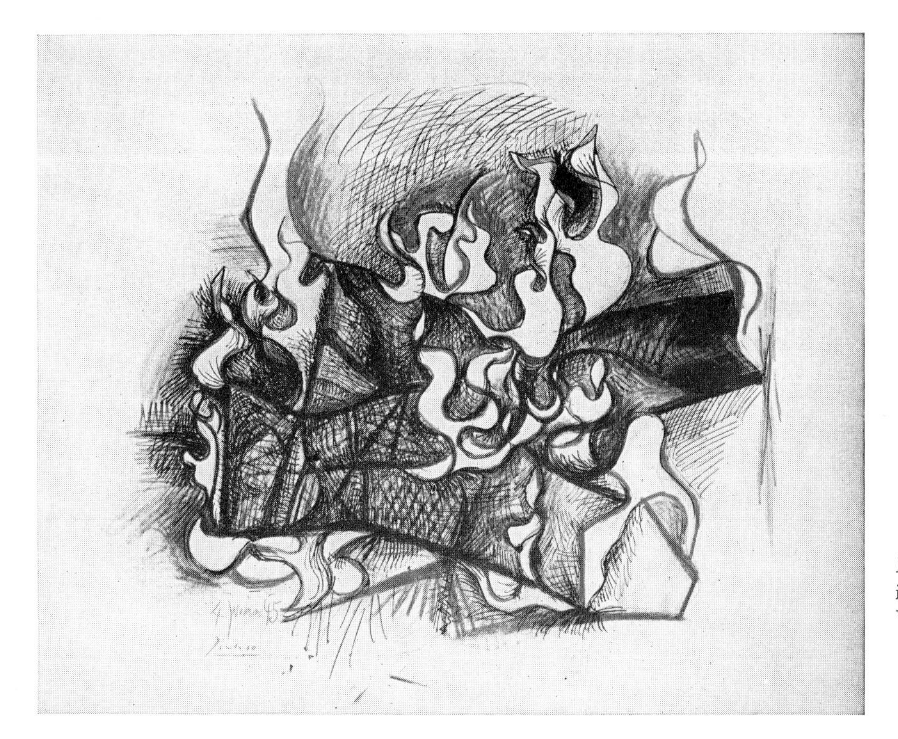

Burning Logs. (Paris) 4 January 1945. Pen and ink with crayon, 19½ x 23½″. Mr. and Mrs. Walter Bareiss, Greenwich, Conn.

1945: 9½″

5½″

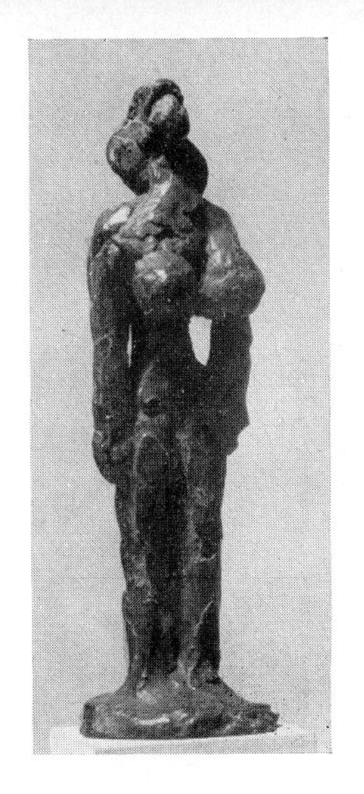

8⅞″

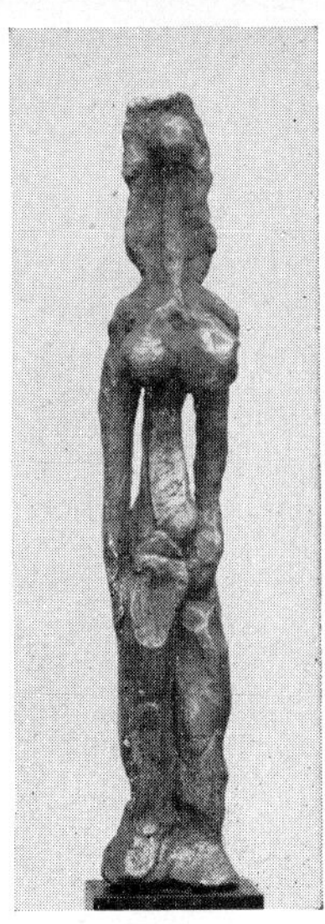

10⅜″

Seventeen small bronzes of female figures, 1945-47, lent by G. David Thompson, Pittsburgh. In the exhibition the bronzes are mounted in two groups of eight and nine each as arranged by the lender. Besides those illustrated here, six bronzes of 1945 are included, measuring 5⅜, 8⅜, 9⅛, 7¼, 10⅛, and 5⅛″ high each; one of 1947, 3⅝″ high; and two duplicate casts.

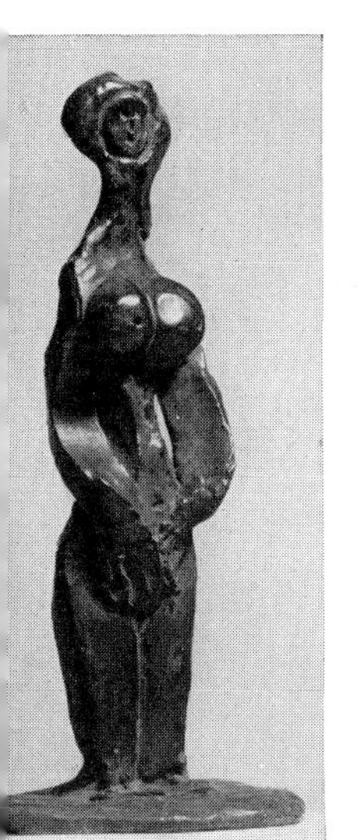

7: 7¾″

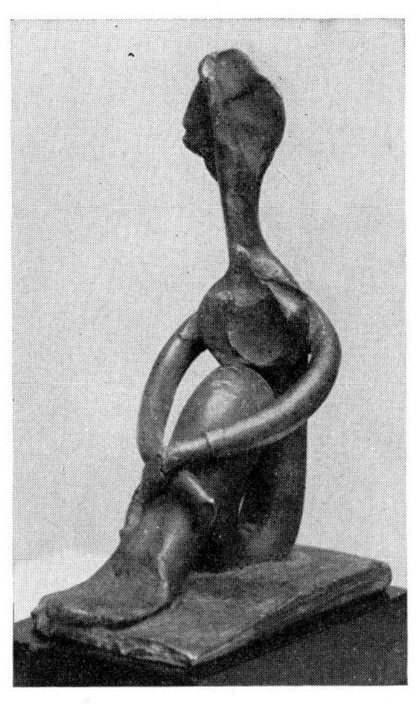

6½″

7¾″

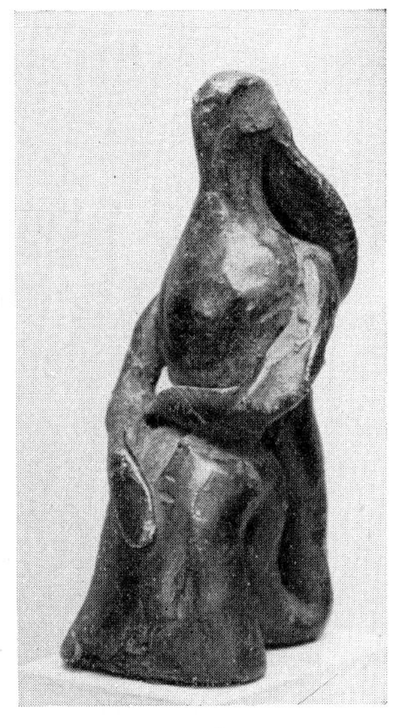

4¾″

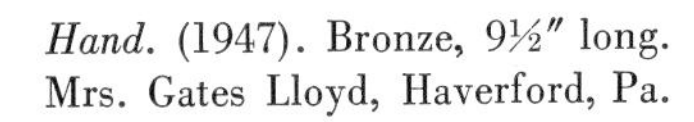

Hand. (1947). Bronze, 9½″ long.
Mrs. Gates Lloyd, Haverford, Pa.

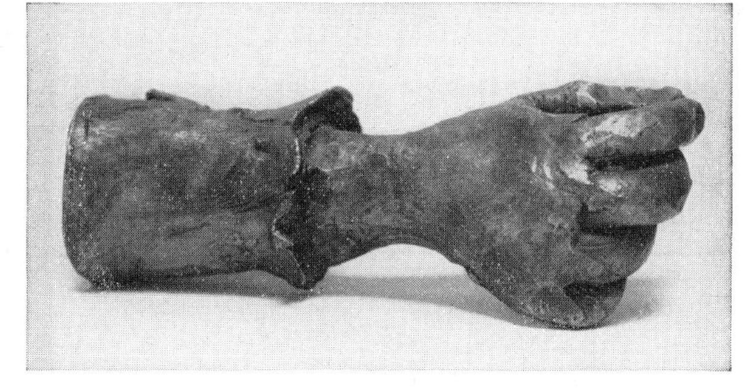

Still Life with Candle. (Paris) 4 April 1944. Oil on canvas, 23⅝ x 36¼″. Jacques Sarlie, New York

Tomato Plant. (Paris) 3 August 1944. Oil on canvas, 28¾ x 36¼″. Guennol Collection, New York

Paris: Notre Dame. 1 March 1945. Oil on canvas, 21¼ x 32″. Herbert and Nannette Rothschild, New York, courtesy Perls Galleries

Above: *Still Life.* (Paris) 20 July 1944. Oil on canvas, 15 x 18½″. Private collection

Left: *The Mirror.* 23 June 1947. Oil on canvas, 24 x 19⅝″. Mr. and Mrs. William A. M. Burden, New York

Seated Woman. 1946. Oil on canvas, 51 x 35″. Mr. and Mrs. Victor W. Ganz, New York

RIGHT, ABOVE: *Pastoral.* (Ménerbes) 22 July 1946. Gouache on paper, 19¾ x 25¾″. Mr. and Mrs. Richard Deutsch, Greenwich, Conn. (Shown in New York only)

RIGHT: *Nymph and Fauns.* (Antibes, 1946). Pencil and watercolor, 19¾ x 25⅞″. Herbert Hemphill, Jr., New York

LEFT: *Portrait of a Painter, after El Greco*. Vallauris, 22 February 1950. Oil on wood, 40 x 32¼″. Siegfried Rosengart, Lucerne

BELOW: *The Kitchen*. (Vallauris) 9 November 1948. Oil on canvas, 68⅞ x 98⅜″. The artist

Winter Landscape. (Vallauris, 22 December 1950). Oil on wood, 40½ x 49½. Mr. and Mrs. Victor W. Ganz, New York

ABOVE: *Chimneys of Vallauris.* 12 January 1951. Oil on canvas, 23⅝ x 28¾″. The artist

LEFT: *Sport of Pages* (or *The Knight*). (Vallauris) 24 February 1951. Oil on canvas, 18⅛ x 24″. The artist

ABOVE: *Claude and Paloma.* Vallauris, 20 January 1950. Oil on wood, 45¾ x 35″. The artist

LEFT: *Claude in Polish Costume.* (Vallauris) 23 October 1948, Oil on canvas, 47⅝ x 19⅝″. The artist

RIGHT: *Paloma Playing.* (Vallauris) 2 February 1950. Oil on wood, 49¼ x 40⅛″. The artist

BELOW: *Paloma Asleep.* Vallauris, 28 December 1952. Oil on wood, 44⅞ x 57½″. The artist

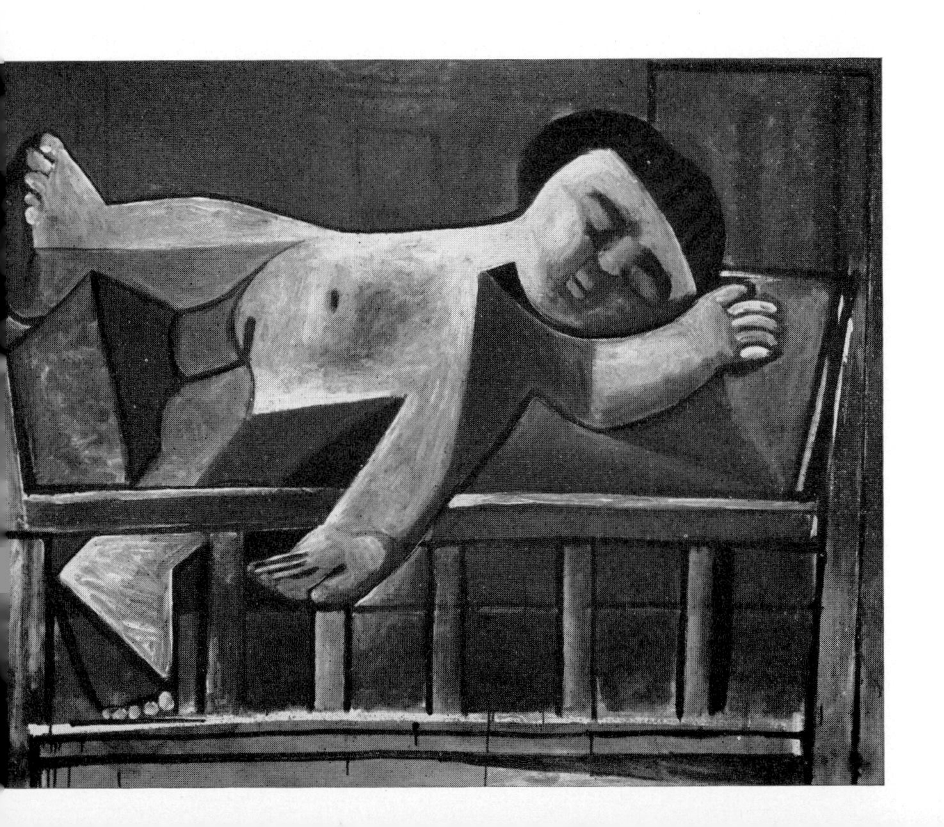

LEFT: *Owl.* (1950). Bronze, 14½″ high. Louis E. Stern, New York

CENTER: *Owl.* 1953. Painted terra cotta, 14″ high. Philip L. Goodwin, New York

RIGHT: *Red and White Owl.* 22 February 1953. Painted terra cotta, 13¾″ high. Nelson A. Rockefeller, New York

ABOVE: *Girl Reading a Book.* (1952-53). Painted bronze, 14″ long. Mr. and Mrs. Gerald Gidwitz, Highland Park, Illinois

LEFT: *Crane.* (1952). Painted bronze, 29¼″ high. G. David Thompson, Pittsburgh

LEFT: *Angry Owl.* (1950). Bronze, 14″ high. Mr. and Mrs. Morton G. Neumann, Chicago

CENTER: *Little Owl.* (1953). Painted bronze, 13″ high. Mr. and Mrs. Victor W. Ganz, New York

RIGHT: *Little Owl.* (1953). Painted bronze, 10¼″ high. Joseph H. Hirshhorn, New York

BELOW LEFT: *Flowers in a Vase.* (1953). Bronze, 29″ high. Mr. and Mrs. Harry Lynde Bradley, Milwaukee

BELOW RIGHT: *Bouquet.* (1953). Bronze, 24″ high. Galerie Louise Leiris, Paris

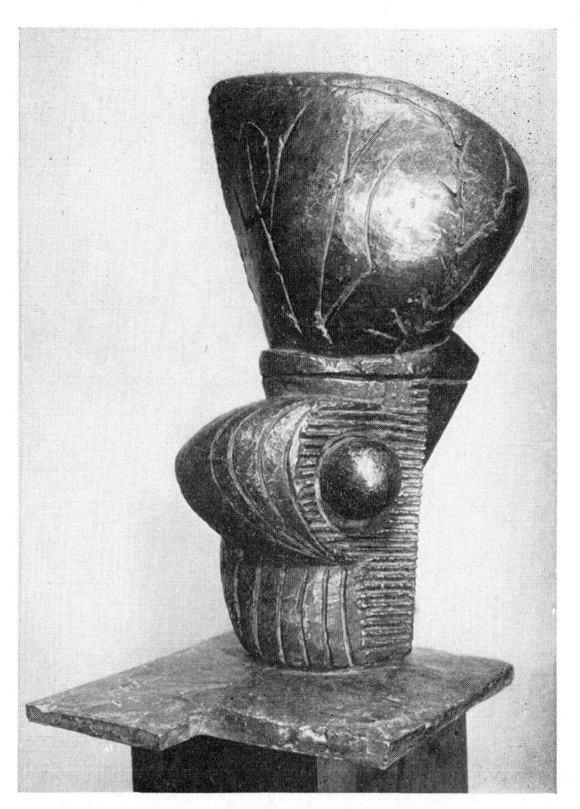

ABOVE: *Woman's Head.* (1951). Bronze, 21⅛″ high. Th[illegible] Museum of Modern Art, New York, Benjamin and Davi[illegible] Scharps Fund

LEFT: *Pregnant Woman.* (1950). Bronze, 41¼″ high. Th[illegible] Museum of Modern Art, New York, gift of Mrs. Louise Smit[illegible]

Right: *Baboon and Young*. 1951. Bronze, 21″ high. The Museum of Modern Art, New York, Mrs. Simon Guggenheim Fund

Below: *Goat Skull and Bottle*. (1951-52). Painted bronze, 31″ high. The Museum of Modern Art, New York, Mrs. Simon Guggenheim Fund

Mme H. P. 4 October 1952. Oil on wood, 57½ x 37¾″. The artist

Mme H. P. Vallauris, 30 July 1952. Oil on wood, 53½ x 41⅜″. The artist

ABOVE: *The Reader.* (Vallauris) 29 January 1953. Oil on wood, 36¼ x 28⅝″. The Art Institute of Chicago, gift of Mr. and Mrs. Arnold H. Maremont through Kate Maremont Foundation

LEFT: *Chinese Commode.* 22 March 1953. Oil on canvas, 57½ x 45″. Saidenberg Gallery, New York

The Studio (*Circus*). 10 January 1954. Brush and ink, 9½ x 12⅝″. Private collection, New York

The Studio (*Visit*). 17 January 1954. Brush and ink, 9½ x 12⅝″. Nelson A. Rockefeller, New York

The Studio (*The Lady Painter*). 21 January 1954. Brush and ink, 9½ x 12⅝″. Mr. and Mrs. Daniel Saidenberg, New York

The Studio (Painter and Model). 24 December 1953. Brush and ink, 12⅝ x 9½″. Mr. and Mrs. Morton G. Neumann, Chicago

The Studio (Models). 21 January 1954. Brush and ink, 9½ x 12⅝″. Nelson A. Rockefeller, New York

The Studio (King and Model). 1 February 1954. Crayon, 9½ x 12⅝″. Mr. and Mrs. Daniel Saidenberg, New York

A

C

E

G

THE WOMEN OF ALGIERS, AFTER DELACROIX

In Paris between December 13, 1954 and February 14, 1955, Picasso painted 15 canvases based upon Delacroix's *Les Femmes d'Alger* (1834) now in the Louvre. The whole series was brought to the United States by Mr. and Mrs. Victor W. Ganz of New York, who retain the final as well as several earlier versions. All 15 have been reassembled for the present exhibition. Of these, nine are illustrated here, the final version, "O," in color, on page 9. The complete series is reproduced in the catalogue of the *Picasso 1955* exhibition, Musée des Arts Décoratifs, Paris, where they were first shown and listed by letter, "A" through "O." All are painted in oil on canvas and dated on the back by the artist.

A 13 December 1954. 23⅝ x 28¾″. Dr. Herschel Carey Walker, New York

B 13 December 1954. 23⅝ x 28¾″. Mr. and Mrs. Wilbur D. May, Reno

C 28 December 1954. 21¼ x 25⅝″. Mr. and Mrs. Victor W. Ganz, New York

D 1 January 1955. 18⅛ x 21⅝″. Paul Rosenberg and Co., New York

H

K

E 16 January 1955. 18⅛ x 21⅝″. Mr. and Mrs. Wilbur D. May, Reno

F 17 January 1955. 21¼ x 25⅝″. Mr. and Mrs. Daniel Saidenberg, New York

G 18 January 1955. 25⅝ x 21¼″. Saidenberg Gallery, New York

H 24 January 1955. 51⅛ x 63¾″. Mr. and Mrs. Victor W. Ganz, New York

I 25 January 1955. 38⅛ x 51⅛″. Paul Rosenberg and Co., New York

J 26 January 1955. 44⅞ x 57½″. Paul Rosenberg and Co., New York

K 6 February 1955. 51⅛ x 63¾″. Mr. and Mrs. Victor W. Ganz, New York

L 9 February 1955. 51⅛ x 38⅛″. Paul Rosenberg and Co., New York

M 11 February 1955. 51¼ x 76¾″. Mr. and Mrs. Victor W. Ganz, New York

N 13 February 1955. 44⅞ x 57½. Paul Rosenberg and Co., New York

O 14 February 1955. 44⅞ x 57½″. Mr. and Mrs. Victor W. Ganz, New York

L

M

N

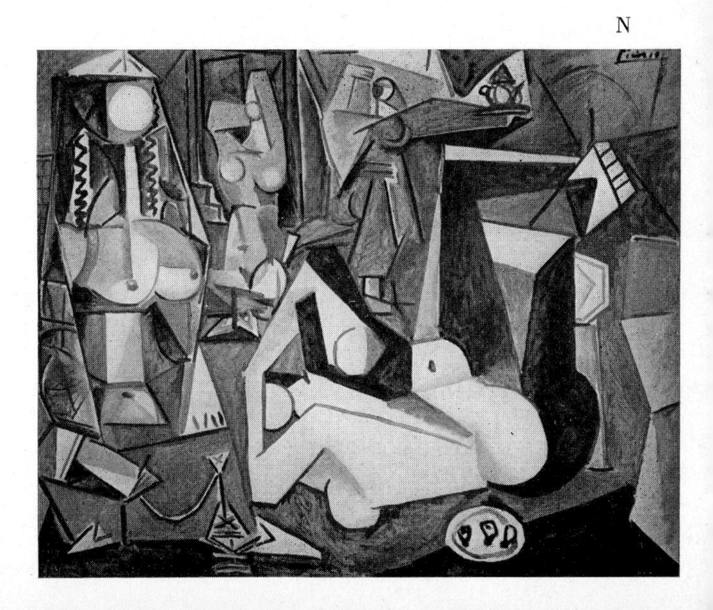

ABOVE: *Portrait of J. R. with Roses.* Vallauris, 2 June 1954. Oil on canvas, 39⅜ x 31⅞". The artist

LEFT: *The Studio.* 24 October 1955. Oil on canvas, 75¾ x 29¾". Saidenberg Gallery, New York

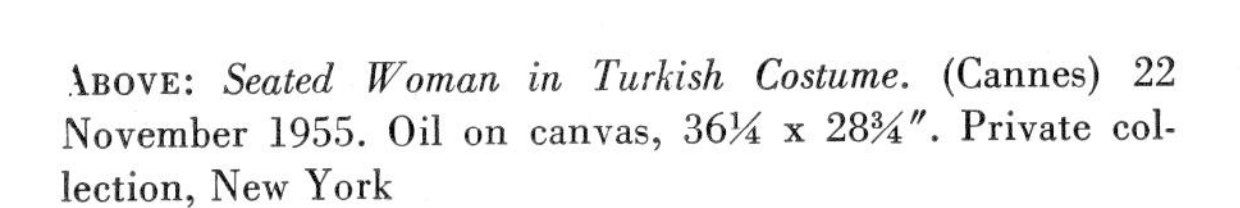

ABOVE: *Seated Woman in Turkish Costume.* (Cannes) 22 November 1955. Oil on canvas, 36¼ x 28¾″. Private collection, New York

RIGHT: *Jardinière with Ferns.* (Cannes) 5 June 1956. Oil on canvas, 63¾ x 51⅛″. Galerie Louise Leiris, Paris

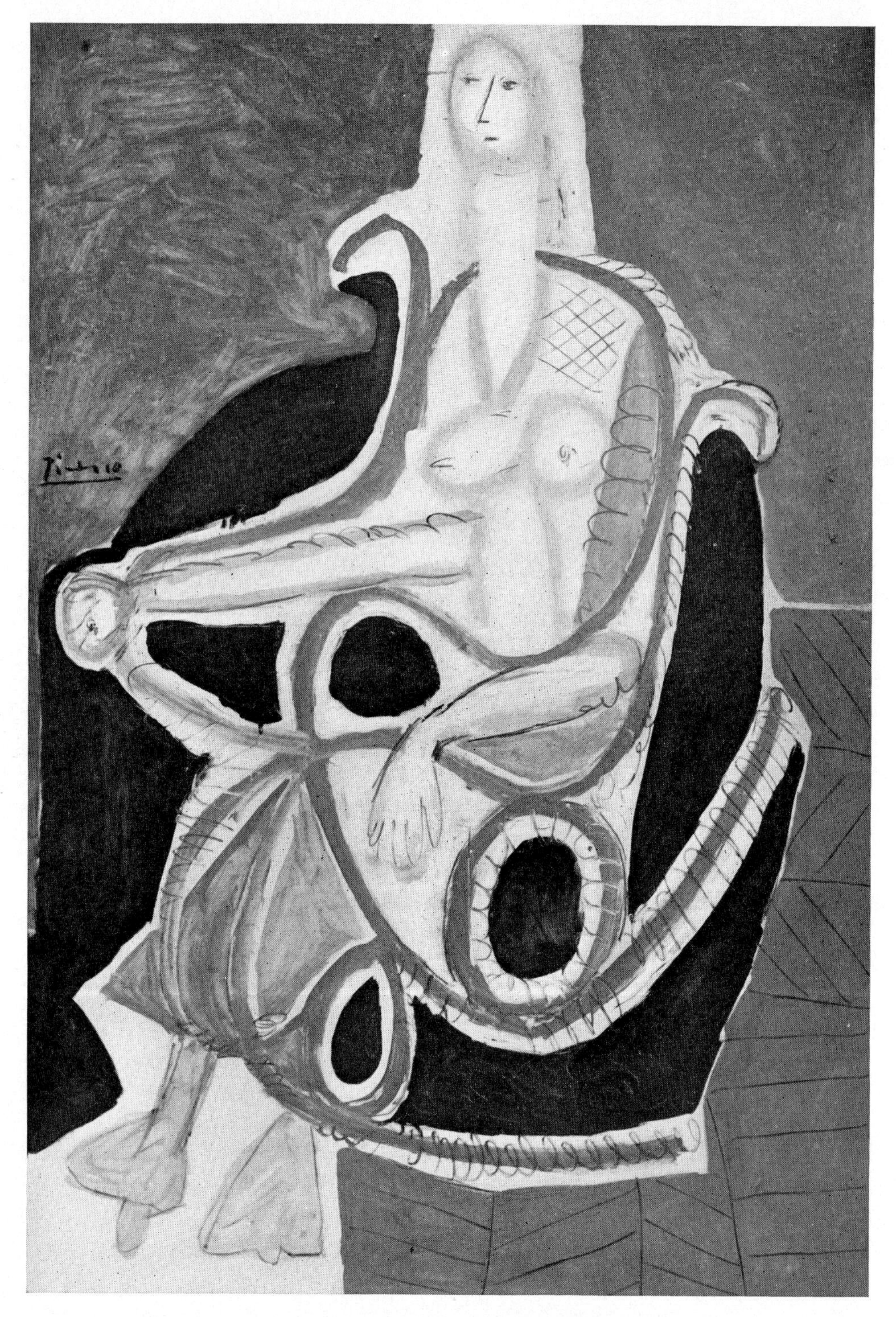

Woman in Rocking Chair. (Cannes) 25 March 1956. Oil on canvas, 75¾ x 51¼". Galerie Louise Leiris, Paris

ABOVE: *The Studio.* (Cannes) 2 April 1956. Oil on canvas, 35 x 45⅝″. Lent anonymously

LEFT: *Bullfight.* (Cannes) 19 May 1956. Oil on canvas, 19⅝ x 24″. Mr. and Mrs. Daniel Saidenberg, New York

Woman by a Window. (Cannes) 11 June 1956. Oil on canvas, 59 x 47¼″. Lent anonymously

ADDENDA

ABOVE: *Man with Pipe.* (Paris) 1915(?) Oil on canvas, 51¼ x 35¼″. The Art Institute of Chicago, gift of Mary L. Block in memory of Albert D. Lasker

LEFT: *Fruit Dish and Pitcher.* (Paris) 21 January 1937. Oil on canvas, 20 x 24″. J. K. Thannhauser, New York

This book has been printed for
the Trustees of the Museum of Modern Art
in May, 1957 by the Plantin Press, New York

The colorplates were manufactured and printed by
J. J. Augustin, Glückstadt, Germany

Cover and title page by Norman Ives